My First Book About Chemistry

Donald M. Silver &
Patricia J. Wynne

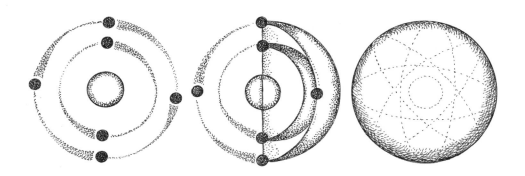

DOVER PUBLICATIONS
Garden City, New York

For Wally Broecker

Our longtime friend, the geology expert who was one of the first scientists to warn the world about the dangers of global warming and who believed in science education for all girls and boys.

What three forms can matter take? Why is the nucleus so important to a cell? How does the stomach break down protein in food? What causes global warming, and what are its effects on the planet? You'll learn many interesting and important facts about chemistry and life on Earth in this exciting book! The easy-to-understand captions and realistic illustrations also explore topics such as chemical energy, thunderstorms, acids and bases, "smell cells," and animal poisons. Plus, you can color each page with colored pencils, crayons, or markers.

Bibliographical Note
My First Book About Chemistry is a new work, first published by Dover Publications in 2020.

International Standard Book Number
ISBN-13: 978-0-486-83758-1
ISBN-10: 0-486-83758-0

Manufactured in the United States of America
83758007   2023
www.doverpublications.com

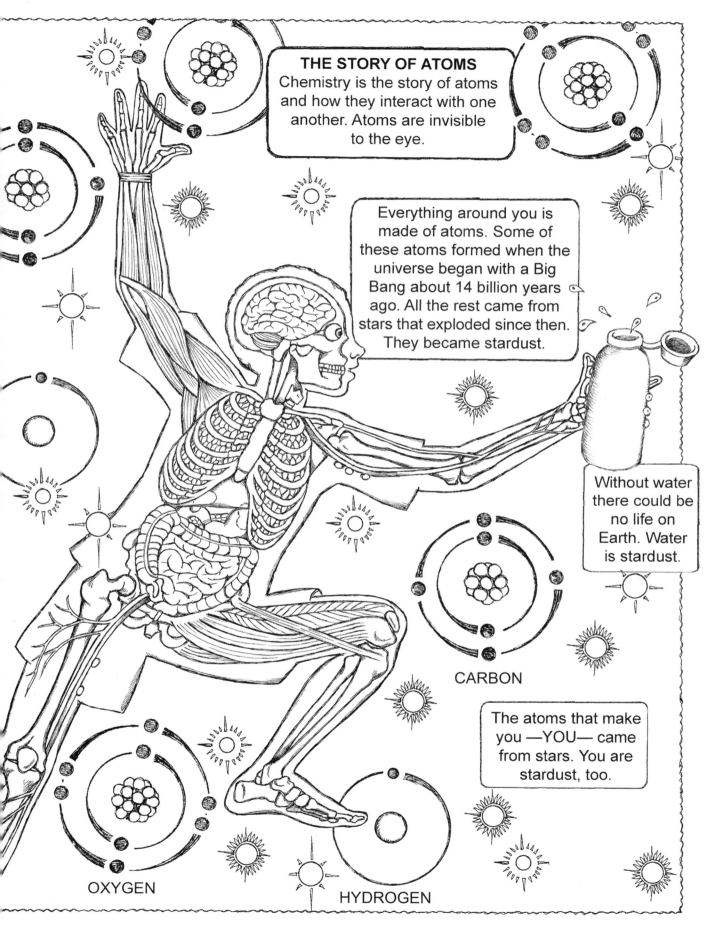

THE STORY OF ATOMS
Chemistry is the story of atoms and how they interact with one another. Atoms are invisible to the eye.

Everything around you is made of atoms. Some of these atoms formed when the universe began with a Big Bang about 14 billion years ago. All the rest came from stars that exploded since then. They became stardust.

Without water there could be no life on Earth. Water is stardust.

CARBON

The atoms that make you —YOU— came from stars. You are stardust, too.

OXYGEN

HYDROGEN

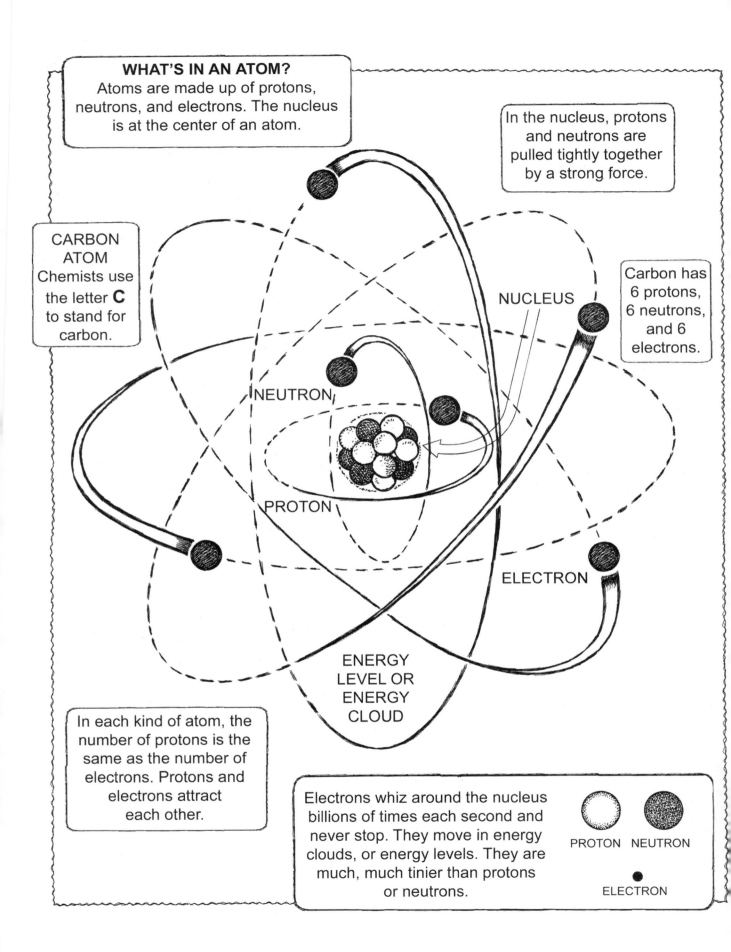

WHAT'S IN AN ATOM?
Atoms are made up of protons, neutrons, and electrons. The nucleus is at the center of an atom.

In the nucleus, protons and neutrons are pulled tightly together by a strong force.

CARBON ATOM
Chemists use the letter **C** to stand for carbon.

Carbon has 6 protons, 6 neutrons, and 6 electrons.

NUCLEUS

NEUTRON

PROTON

ELECTRON

ENERGY LEVEL OR ENERGY CLOUD

In each kind of atom, the number of protons is the same as the number of electrons. Protons and electrons attract each other.

Electrons whiz around the nucleus billions of times each second and never stop. They move in energy clouds, or energy levels. They are much, much tinier than protons or neutrons.

PROTON   NEUTRON

ELECTRON

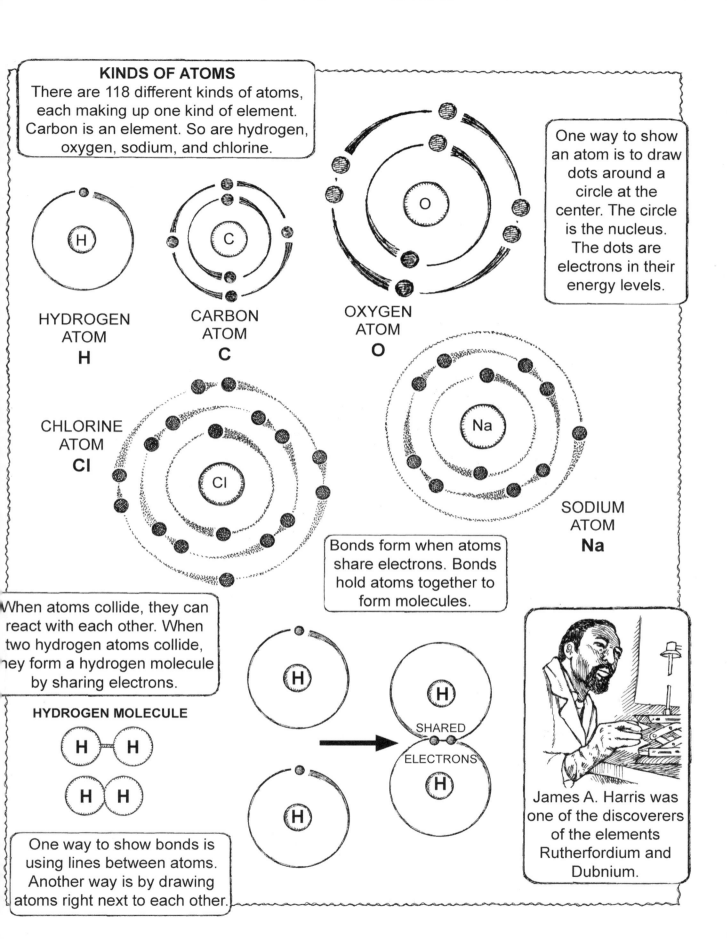

KINDS OF ATOMS
There are 118 different kinds of atoms, each making up one kind of element. Carbon is an element. So are hydrogen, oxygen, sodium, and chlorine.

One way to show an atom is to draw dots around a circle at the center. The circle is the nucleus. The dots are electrons in their energy levels.

HYDROGEN ATOM
H

CARBON ATOM
C

OXYGEN ATOM
O

CHLORINE ATOM
Cl

SODIUM ATOM
Na

Bonds form when atoms share electrons. Bonds hold atoms together to form molecules.

When atoms collide, they can react with each other. When two hydrogen atoms collide, they form a hydrogen molecule by sharing electrons.

HYDROGEN MOLECULE

H H

H H

SHARED ELECTRONS

One way to show bonds is using lines between atoms. Another way is by drawing atoms right next to each other.

James A. Harris was one of the discoverers of the elements Rutherfordium and Dubnium.

MAKING WATER

Hydrogen is a gas. Oxygen is a gas, too. Mix them together and supply the right energy, like a spark, and liquid water forms.

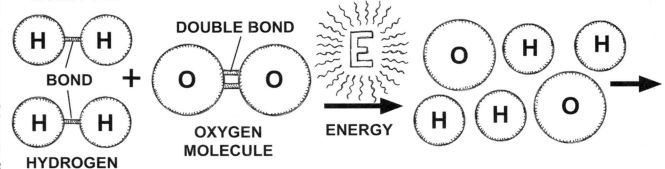

HYDROGEN MOLECULE

BOND

HYDROGEN MOLECULE

DOUBLE BOND

OXYGEN MOLECULE

ENERGY

1 To make two molecules of water, it takes two hydrogen molecules and one oxygen molecule.

2 When the hydrogen and oxygen bonds break, the atoms rearrange and new bonds form in each water molecule. None of the atoms disappear.

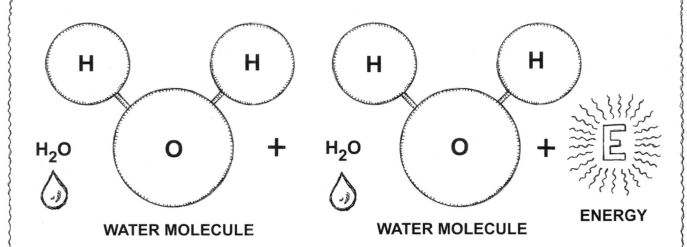

H_2O

WATER MOLECULE

H_2O

WATER MOLECULE

ENERGY

3 A molecule of water is made of two hydrogen atoms sharing electrons with one oxygen atom. Because it contains two or more elements joined together, water is a compound.

4

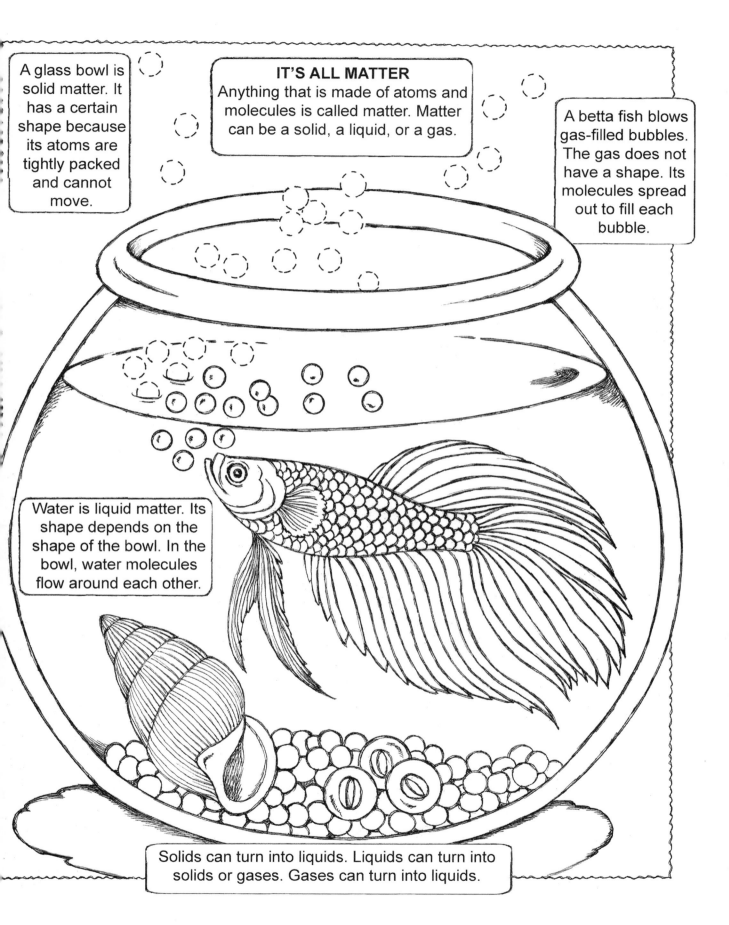

A glass bowl is solid matter. It has a certain shape because its atoms are tightly packed and cannot move.

IT'S ALL MATTER
Anything that is made of atoms and molecules is called matter. Matter can be a solid, a liquid, or a gas.

A betta fish blows gas-filled bubbles. The gas does not have a shape. Its molecules spread out to fill each bubble.

Water is liquid matter. Its shape depends on the shape of the bowl. In the bowl, water molecules flow around each other.

Solids can turn into liquids. Liquids can turn into solids or gases. Gases can turn into liquids.

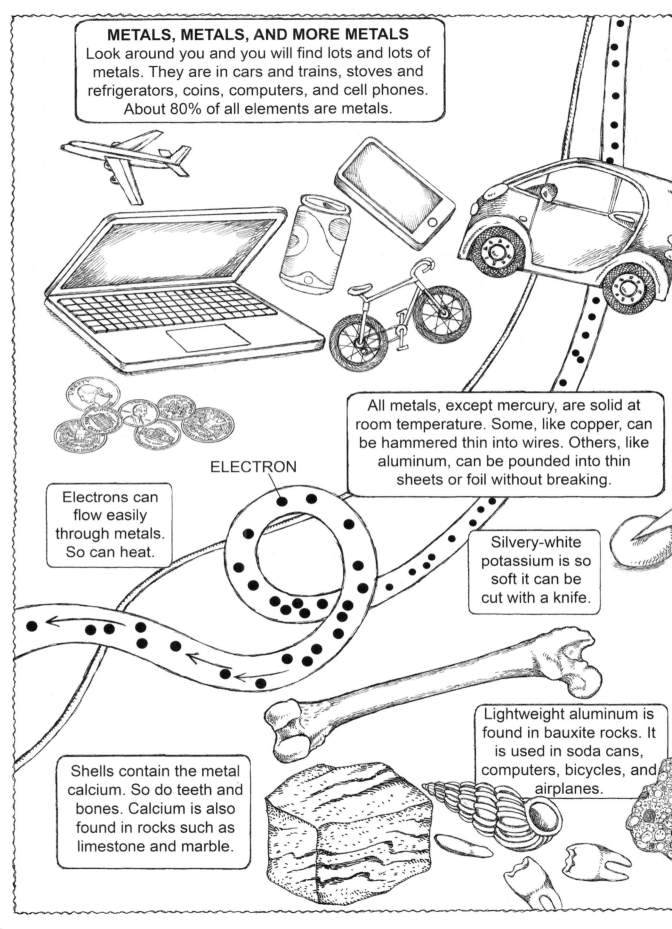

METALS, METALS, AND MORE METALS
Look around you and you will find lots and lots of metals. They are in cars and trains, stoves and refrigerators, coins, computers, and cell phones. About 80% of all elements are metals.

All metals, except mercury, are solid at room temperature. Some, like copper, can be hammered thin into wires. Others, like aluminum, can be pounded into thin sheets or foil without breaking.

ELECTRON

Electrons can flow easily through metals. So can heat.

Silvery-white potassium is so soft it can be cut with a knife.

Lightweight aluminum is found in bauxite rocks. It is used in soda cans, computers, bicycles, and airplanes.

Shells contain the metal calcium. So do teeth and bones. Calcium is also found in rocks such as limestone and marble.

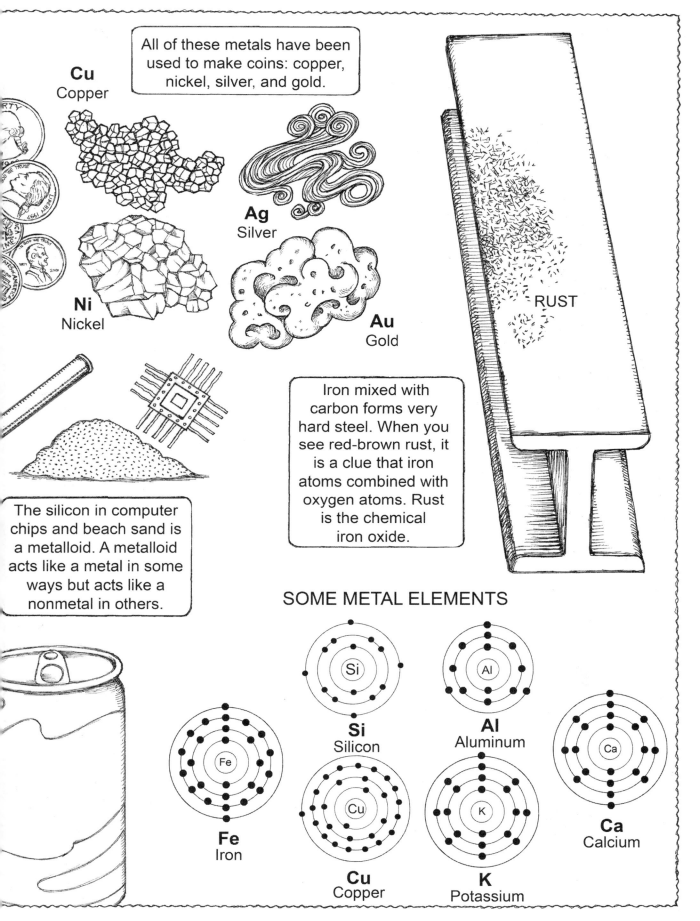

Cu
Copper

All of these metals have been used to make coins: copper, nickel, silver, and gold.

Ag
Silver

Ni
Nickel

Au
Gold

RUST

Iron mixed with carbon forms very hard steel. When you see red-brown rust, it is a clue that iron atoms combined with oxygen atoms. Rust is the chemical iron oxide.

The silicon in computer chips and beach sand is a metalloid. A metalloid acts like a metal in some ways but acts like a nonmetal in others.

SOME METAL ELEMENTS

Si
Silicon

Al
Aluminum

Ca
Calcium

Fe
Iron

Cu
Copper

K
Potassium

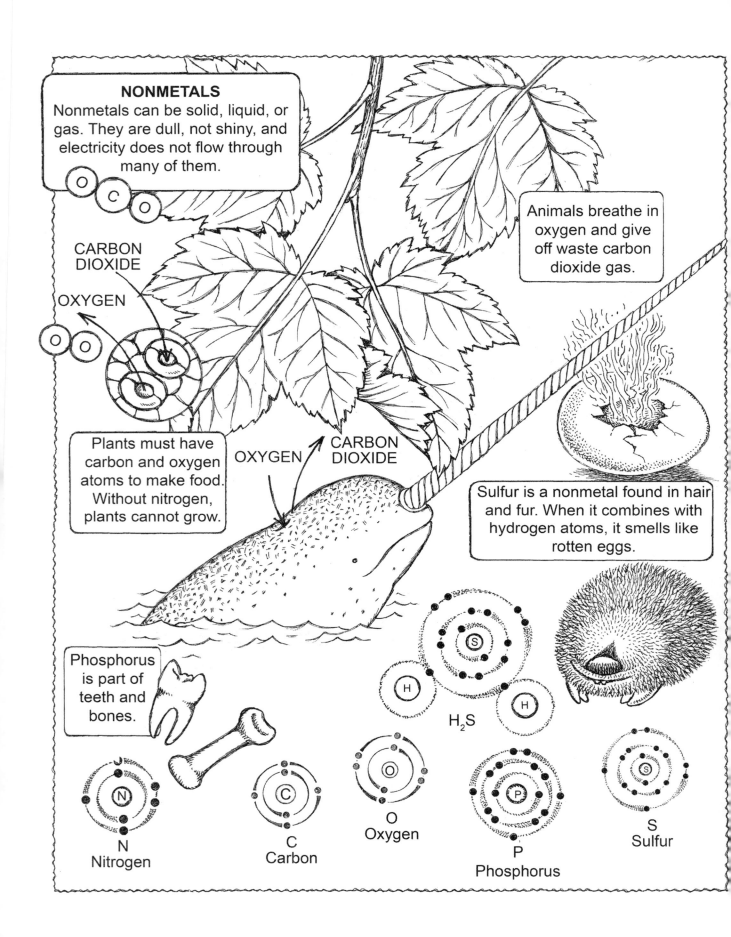

NONMETALS

Nonmetals can be solid, liquid, or gas. They are dull, not shiny, and electricity does not flow through many of them.

CARBON DIOXIDE

OXYGEN

Plants must have carbon and oxygen atoms to make food. Without nitrogen, plants cannot grow.

OXYGEN

CARBON DIOXIDE

Animals breathe in oxygen and give off waste carbon dioxide gas.

Sulfur is a nonmetal found in hair and fur. When it combines with hydrogen atoms, it smells like rotten eggs.

Phosphorus is part of teeth and bones.

H_2S

N
Nitrogen

C
Carbon

O
Oxygen

P
Phosphorus

S
Sulfur

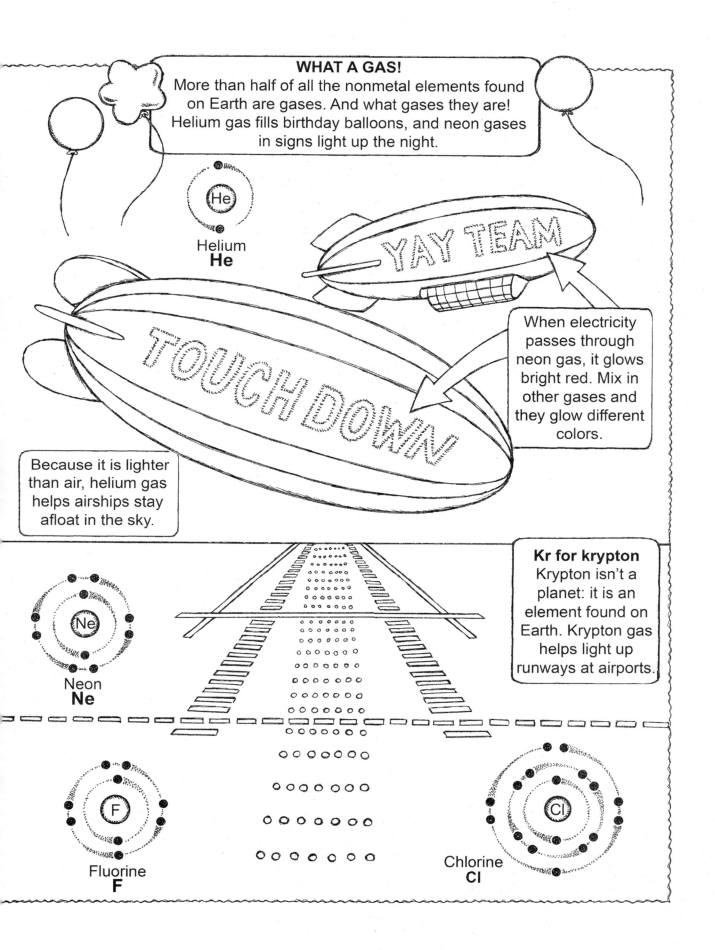

WHAT A GAS!
More than half of all the nonmetal elements found on Earth are gases. And what gases they are! Helium gas fills birthday balloons, and neon gases in signs light up the night.

Helium
He

YAY TEAM

TOUCH DOWN

When electricity passes through neon gas, it glows bright red. Mix in other gases and they glow different colors.

Because it is lighter than air, helium gas helps airships stay afloat in the sky.

Kr for krypton
Krypton isn't a planet: it is an element found on Earth. Krypton gas helps light up runways at airports.

Neon
Ne

Fluorine
F

Chlorine
Cl

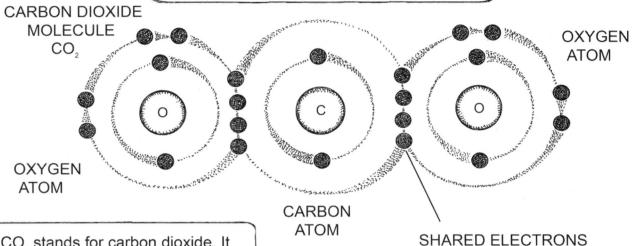

CARBON DIOXIDE MOLECULE CO_2

OXYGEN ATOM

OXYGEN ATOM

CARBON ATOM

SHARED ELECTRONS

CO_2 stands for carbon dioxide. It means a molecule of carbon dioxide has one carbon atom and two oxygen atoms.

When carbon combines with oxygen, the two atoms share electrons. They form bonds that hold carbon dioxide together.

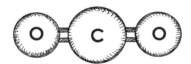

When coal burns in the air, carbon atoms combine with oxygen to form the gas called carbon dioxide. Heat and light energy are also given off.

COAL

Coal is a fuel that is made mostly of carbon. It formed hundreds of millions of years ago from layers of partly rotted plants that grew in swampy forests.

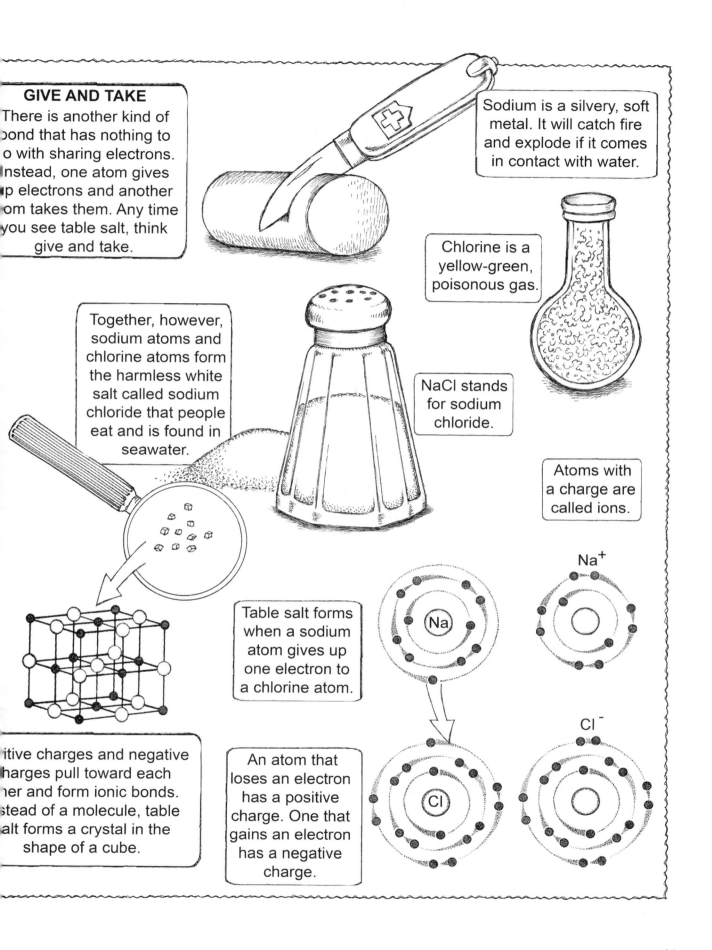

GIVE AND TAKE

There is another kind of bond that has nothing to do with sharing electrons. Instead, one atom gives up electrons and another atom takes them. Any time you see table salt, think give and take.

Sodium is a silvery, soft metal. It will catch fire and explode if it comes in contact with water.

Chlorine is a yellow-green, poisonous gas.

Together, however, sodium atoms and chlorine atoms form the harmless white salt called sodium chloride that people eat and is found in seawater.

NaCl stands for sodium chloride.

Atoms with a charge are called ions.

Na$^+$

Positive charges and negative charges pull toward each other and form ionic bonds. Instead of a molecule, table salt forms a crystal in the shape of a cube.

Table salt forms when a sodium atom gives up one electron to a chlorine atom.

Na

An atom that loses an electron has a positive charge. One that gains an electron has a negative charge.

Cl$^-$

Cl

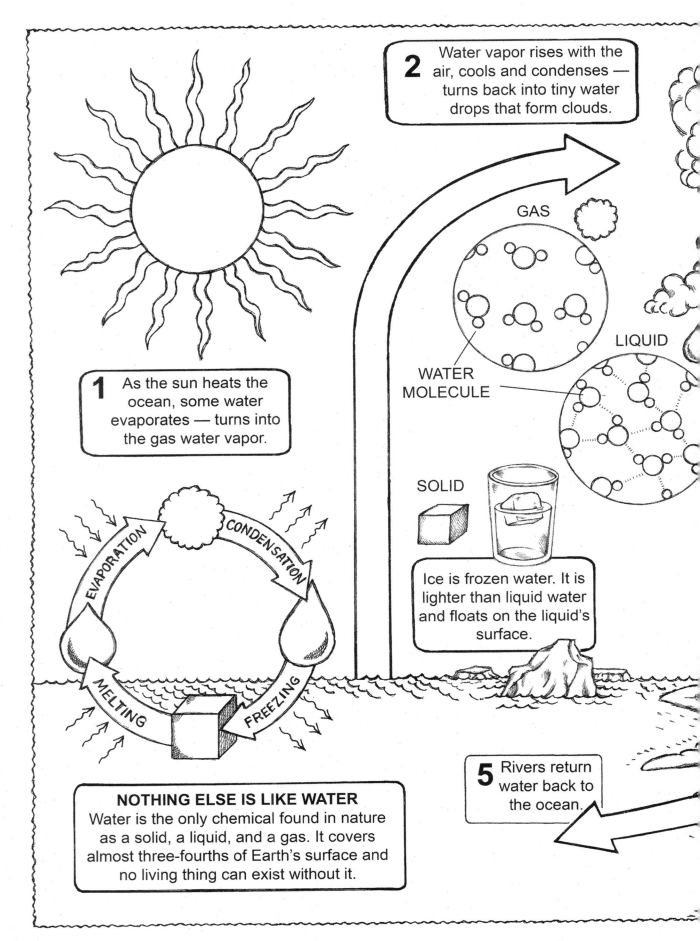

2 Water vapor rises with the air, cools and condenses — turns back into tiny water drops that form clouds.

GAS

WATER MOLECULE

LIQUID

SOLID

Ice is frozen water. It is lighter than liquid water and floats on the liquid's surface.

1 As the sun heats the ocean, some water evaporates — turns into the gas water vapor.

EVAPORATION

CONDENSATION

MELTING

FREEZING

NOTHING ELSE IS LIKE WATER
Water is the only chemical found in nature as a solid, a liquid, and a gas. It covers almost three-fourths of Earth's surface and no living thing can exist without it.

5 Rivers return water back to the ocean.

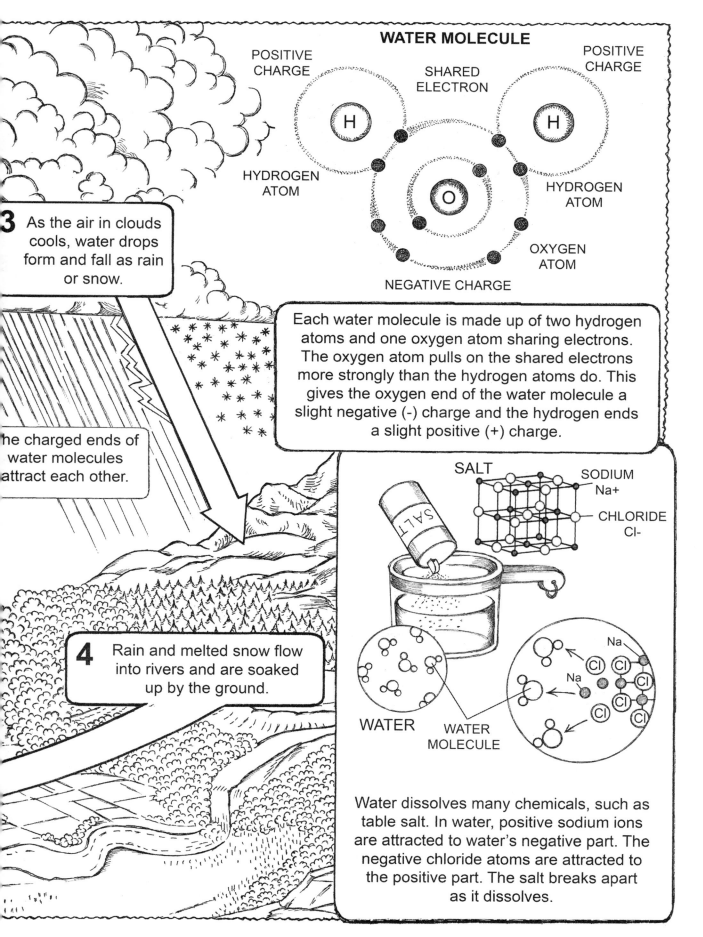

WATER MOLECULE

POSITIVE CHARGE

SHARED ELECTRON

POSITIVE CHARGE

H

H

HYDROGEN ATOM

HYDROGEN ATOM

O

OXYGEN ATOM

NEGATIVE CHARGE

3 As the air in clouds cools, water drops form and fall as rain or snow.

Each water molecule is made up of two hydrogen atoms and one oxygen atom sharing electrons. The oxygen atom pulls on the shared electrons more strongly than the hydrogen atoms do. This gives the oxygen end of the water molecule a slight negative (-) charge and the hydrogen ends a slight positive (+) charge.

The charged ends of water molecules attract each other.

SALT

SODIUM Na+

CHLORIDE Cl-

4 Rain and melted snow flow into rivers and are soaked up by the ground.

WATER

WATER MOLECULE

Na

Cl Cl

Na

Cl

Cl

Cl Cl

Water dissolves many chemicals, such as table salt. In water, positive sodium ions are attracted to water's negative part. The negative chloride atoms are attracted to the positive part. The salt breaks apart as it dissolves.

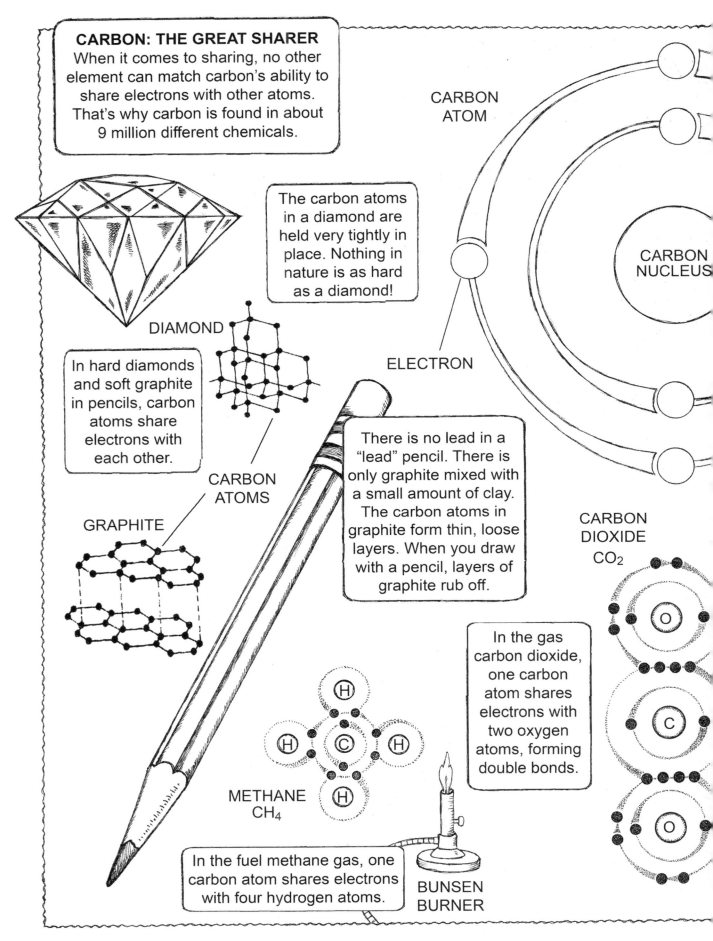

CARBON: THE GREAT SHARER
When it comes to sharing, no other element can match carbon's ability to share electrons with other atoms. That's why carbon is found in about 9 million different chemicals.

CARBON ATOM

The carbon atoms in a diamond are held very tightly in place. Nothing in nature is as hard as a diamond!

CARBON NUCLEUS

DIAMOND

In hard diamonds and soft graphite in pencils, carbon atoms share electrons with each other.

ELECTRON

CARBON ATOMS

There is no lead in a "lead" pencil. There is only graphite mixed with a small amount of clay. The carbon atoms in graphite form thin, loose layers. When you draw with a pencil, layers of graphite rub off.

GRAPHITE

CARBON DIOXIDE CO_2

In the gas carbon dioxide, one carbon atom shares electrons with two oxygen atoms, forming double bonds.

METHANE CH_4

In the fuel methane gas, one carbon atom shares electrons with four hydrogen atoms.

BUNSEN BURNER

14

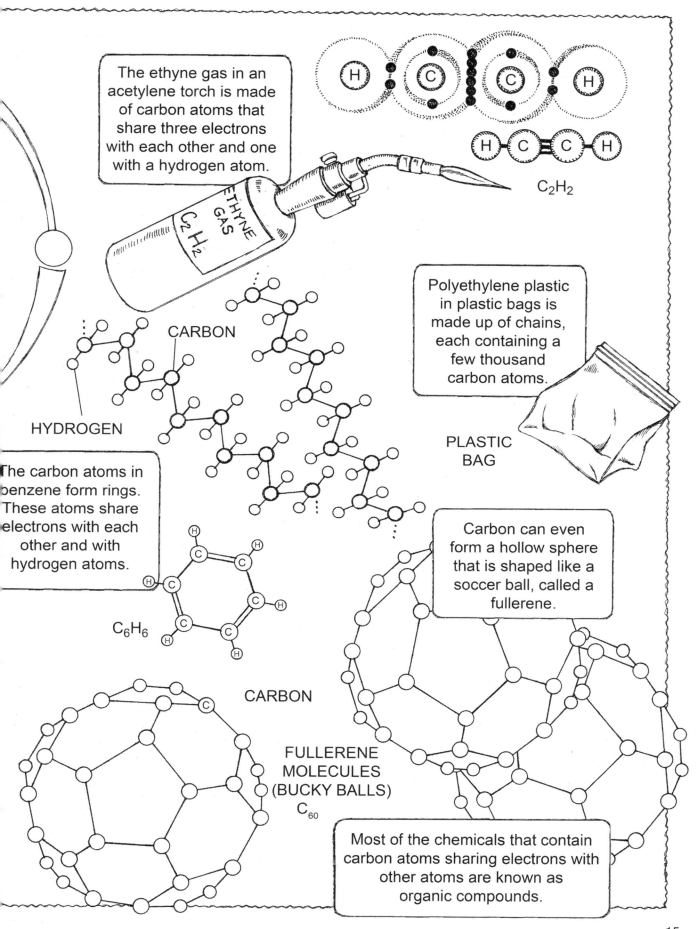

The ethyne gas in an acetylene torch is made of carbon atoms that share three electrons with each other and one with a hydrogen atom.

C_2H_2

ETHYNE GAS C_2H_2

CARBON

HYDROGEN

Polyethylene plastic in plastic bags is made up of chains, each containing a few thousand carbon atoms.

PLASTIC BAG

The carbon atoms in benzene form rings. These atoms share electrons with each other and with hydrogen atoms.

C_6H_6

Carbon can even form a hollow sphere that is shaped like a soccer ball, called a fullerene.

CARBON

FULLERENE MOLECULES (BUCKY BALLS) C_{60}

Most of the chemicals that contain carbon atoms sharing electrons with other atoms are known as organic compounds.

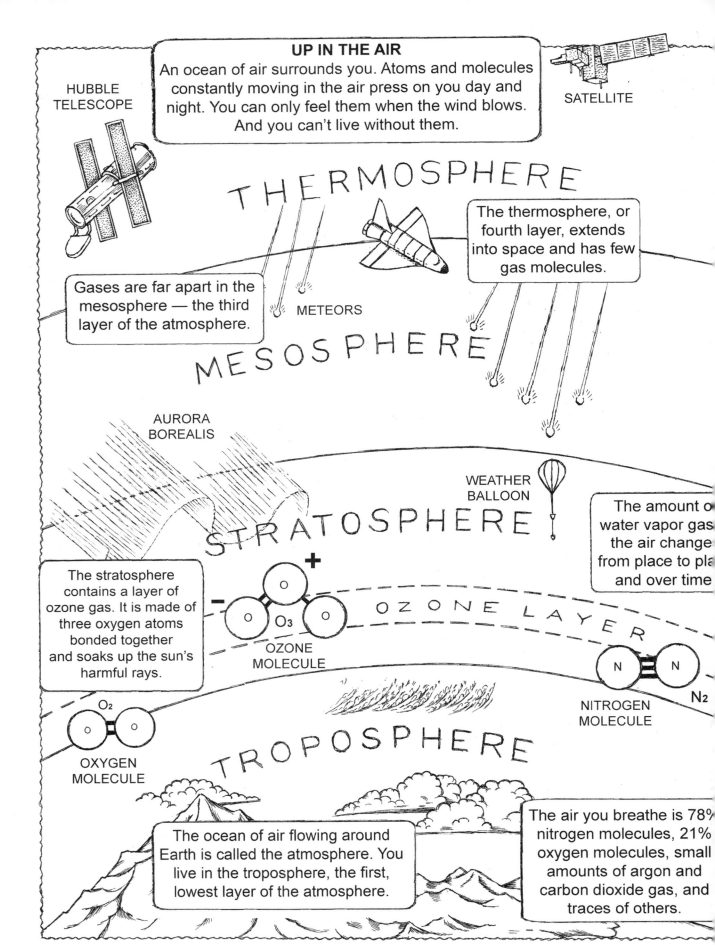

UP IN THE AIR
An ocean of air surrounds you. Atoms and molecules constantly moving in the air press on you day and night. You can only feel them when the wind blows. And you can't live without them.

HUBBLE TELESCOPE

SATELLITE

THERMOSPHERE

The thermosphere, or fourth layer, extends into space and has few gas molecules.

Gases are far apart in the mesosphere — the third layer of the atmosphere.

METEORS

MESOSPHERE

AURORA BOREALIS

WEATHER BALLOON

STRATOSPHERE

The amount o water vapor gas the air change from place to pla and over time

The stratosphere contains a layer of ozone gas. It is made of three oxygen atoms bonded together and soaks up the sun's harmful rays.

+
−
O
O O_3 O

OZONE MOLECULE

OZONE LAYER

N   N

N_2

NITROGEN MOLECULE

O_2
O   O

OXYGEN MOLECULE

TROPOSPHERE

The ocean of air flowing around Earth is called the atmosphere. You live in the troposphere, the first, lowest layer of the atmosphere.

The air you breathe is 78% nitrogen molecules, 21% oxygen molecules, small amounts of argon and carbon dioxide gas, and traces of others.

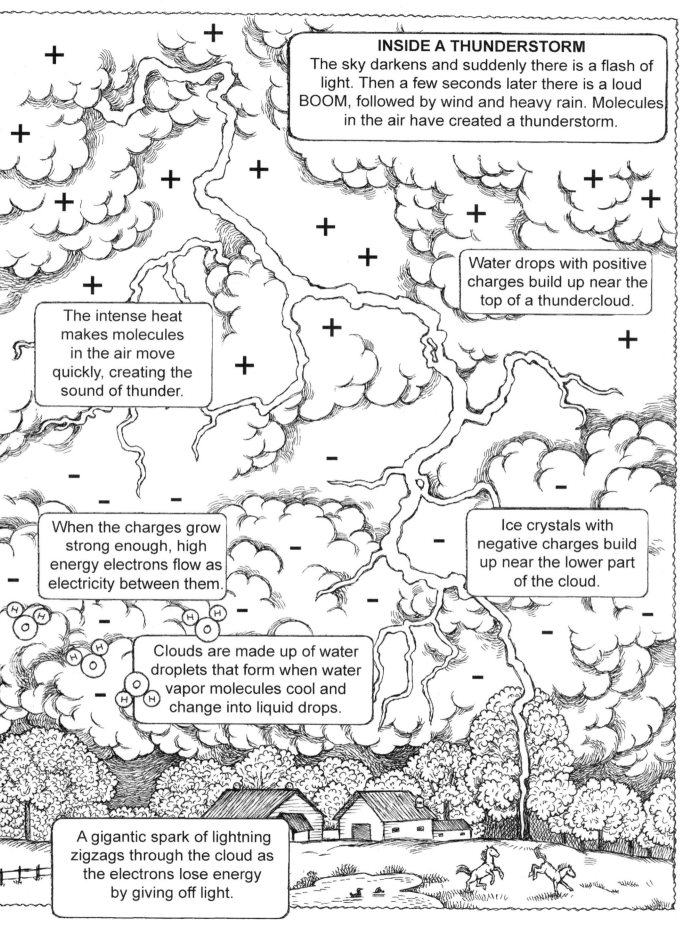

INSIDE A THUNDERSTORM
The sky darkens and suddenly there is a flash of light. Then a few seconds later there is a loud BOOM, followed by wind and heavy rain. Molecules in the air have created a thunderstorm.

Water drops with positive charges build up near the top of a thundercloud.

The intense heat makes molecules in the air move quickly, creating the sound of thunder.

When the charges grow strong enough, high energy electrons flow as electricity between them.

Ice crystals with negative charges build up near the lower part of the cloud.

Clouds are made up of water droplets that form when water vapor molecules cool and change into liquid drops.

A gigantic spark of lightning zigzags through the cloud as the electrons lose energy by giving off light.

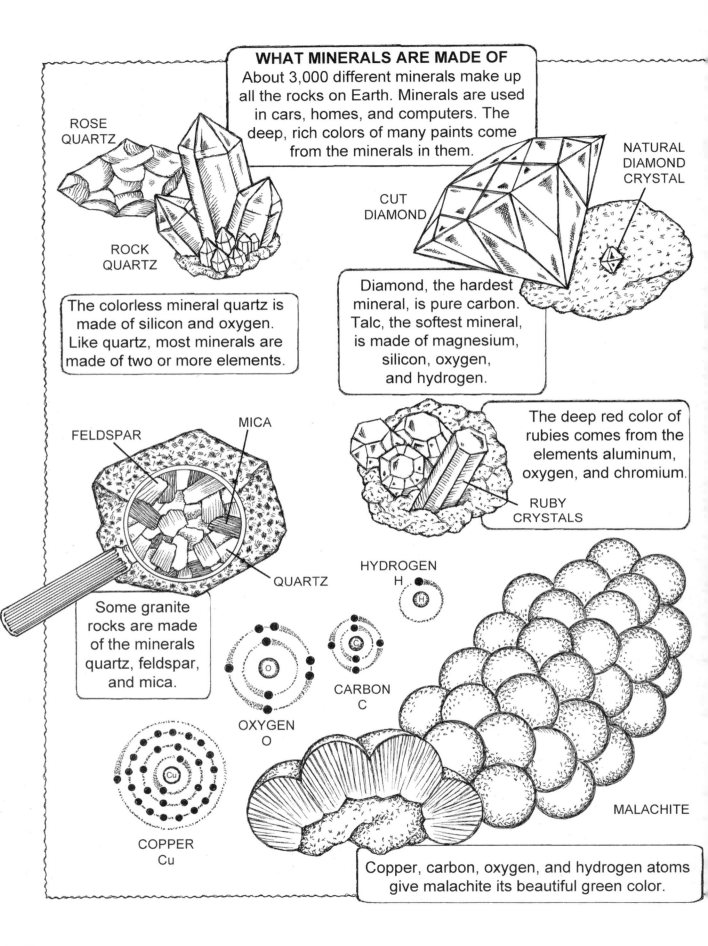

WHAT MINERALS ARE MADE OF
About 3,000 different minerals make up all the rocks on Earth. Minerals are used in cars, homes, and computers. The deep, rich colors of many paints come from the minerals in them.

ROSE QUARTZ

ROCK QUARTZ

CUT DIAMOND

NATURAL DIAMOND CRYSTAL

The colorless mineral quartz is made of silicon and oxygen. Like quartz, most minerals are made of two or more elements.

Diamond, the hardest mineral, is pure carbon. Talc, the softest mineral, is made of magnesium, silicon, oxygen, and hydrogen.

FELDSPAR

MICA

The deep red color of rubies comes from the elements aluminum, oxygen, and chromium.

RUBY CRYSTALS

QUARTZ

HYDROGEN
H

Some granite rocks are made of the minerals quartz, feldspar, and mica.

OXYGEN
O

CARBON
C

COPPER
Cu

MALACHITE

Copper, carbon, oxygen, and hydrogen atoms give malachite its beautiful green color.

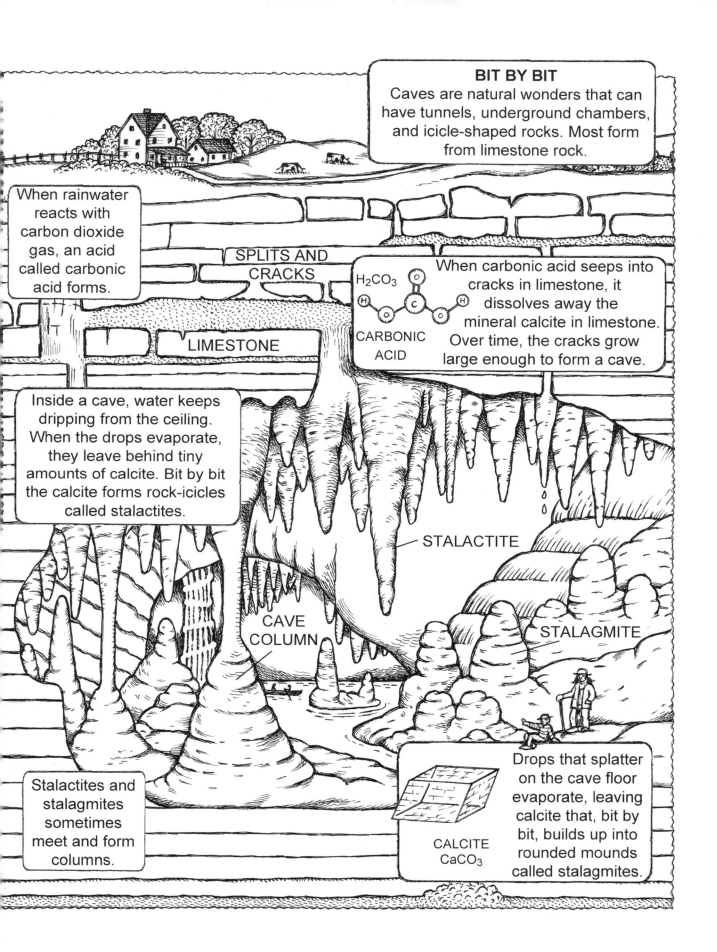

BIT BY BIT
Caves are natural wonders that can have tunnels, underground chambers, and icicle-shaped rocks. Most form from limestone rock.

When rainwater reacts with carbon dioxide gas, an acid called carbonic acid forms.

SPLITS AND CRACKS

H_2CO_3

CARBONIC ACID

When carbonic acid seeps into cracks in limestone, it dissolves away the mineral calcite in limestone. Over time, the cracks grow large enough to form a cave.

LIMESTONE

Inside a cave, water keeps dripping from the ceiling. When the drops evaporate, they leave behind tiny amounts of calcite. Bit by bit the calcite forms rock-icicles called stalactites.

STALACTITE

CAVE COLUMN

STALAGMITE

Stalactites and stalagmites sometimes meet and form columns.

CALCITE $CaCO_3$

Drops that splatter on the cave floor evaporate, leaving calcite that, bit by bit, builds up into rounded mounds called stalagmites.

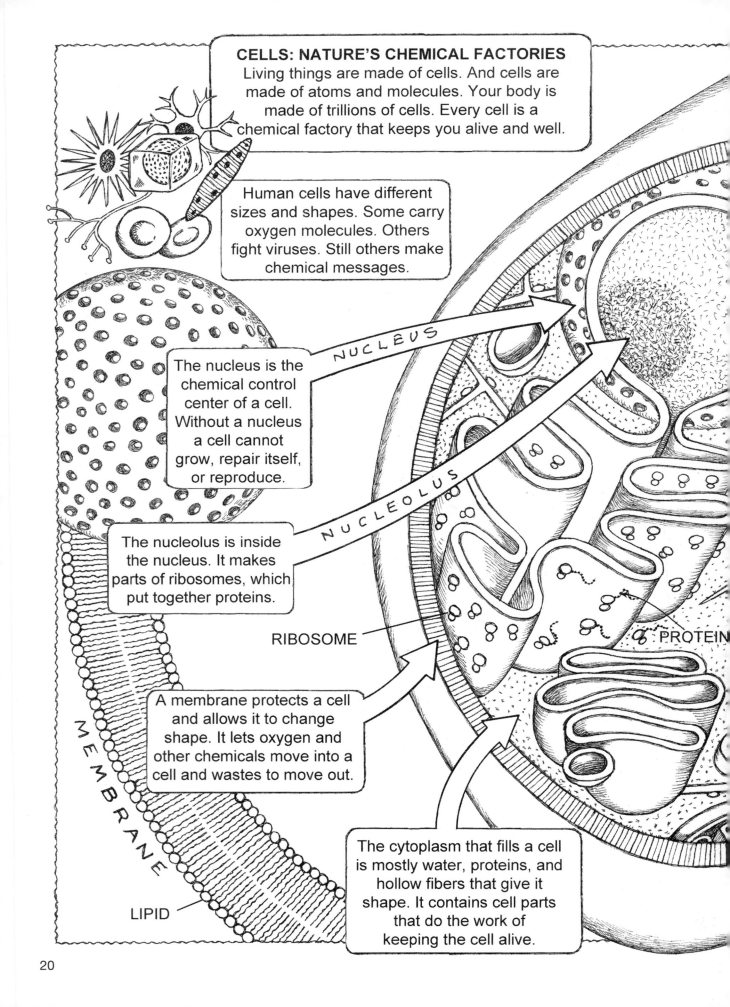

CELLS: NATURE'S CHEMICAL FACTORIES
Living things are made of cells. And cells are made of atoms and molecules. Your body is made of trillions of cells. Every cell is a chemical factory that keeps you alive and well.

Human cells have different sizes and shapes. Some carry oxygen molecules. Others fight viruses. Still others make chemical messages.

NUCLEUS

The nucleus is the chemical control center of a cell. Without a nucleus a cell cannot grow, repair itself, or reproduce.

NUCLEOLUS

The nucleolus is inside the nucleus. It makes parts of ribosomes, which put together proteins.

RIBOSOME

PROTEIN

A membrane protects a cell and allows it to change shape. It lets oxygen and other chemicals move into a cell and wastes to move out.

The cytoplasm that fills a cell is mostly water, proteins, and hollow fibers that give it shape. It contains cell parts that do the work of keeping the cell alive.

MEMBRANE

LIPID

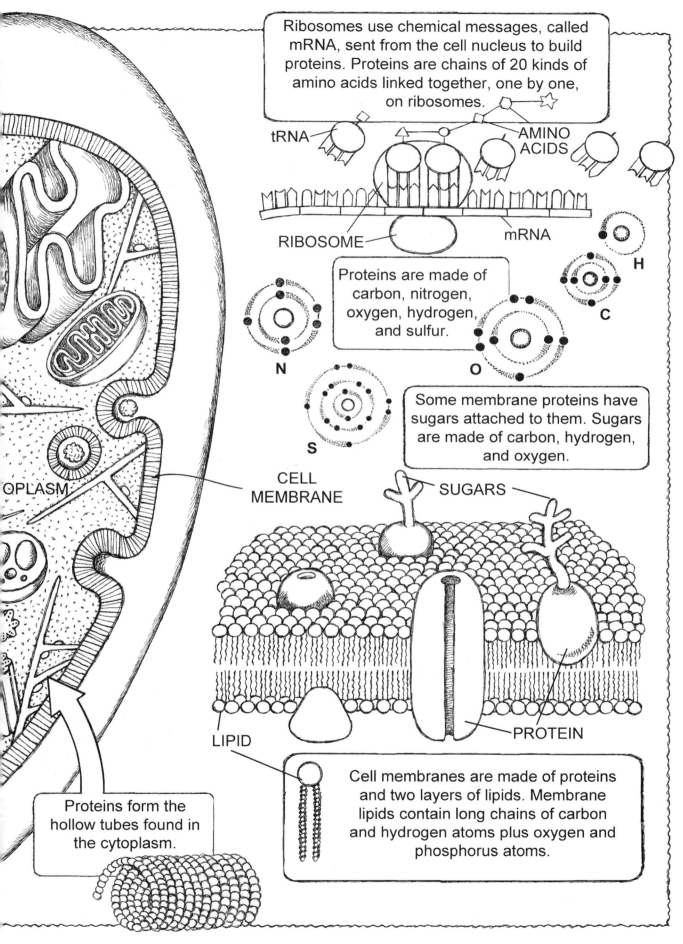

Ribosomes use chemical messages, called mRNA, sent from the cell nucleus to build proteins. Proteins are chains of 20 kinds of amino acids linked together, one by one, on ribosomes.

tRNA

AMINO ACIDS

RIBOSOME

mRNA

H

C

Proteins are made of carbon, nitrogen, oxygen, hydrogen, and sulfur.

N

O

S

Some membrane proteins have sugars attached to them. Sugars are made of carbon, hydrogen, and oxygen.

OPLASM

CELL MEMBRANE

SUGARS

LIPID

PROTEIN

Proteins form the hollow tubes found in the cytoplasm.

Cell membranes are made of proteins and two layers of lipids. Membrane lipids contain long chains of carbon and hydrogen atoms plus oxygen and phosphorus atoms.

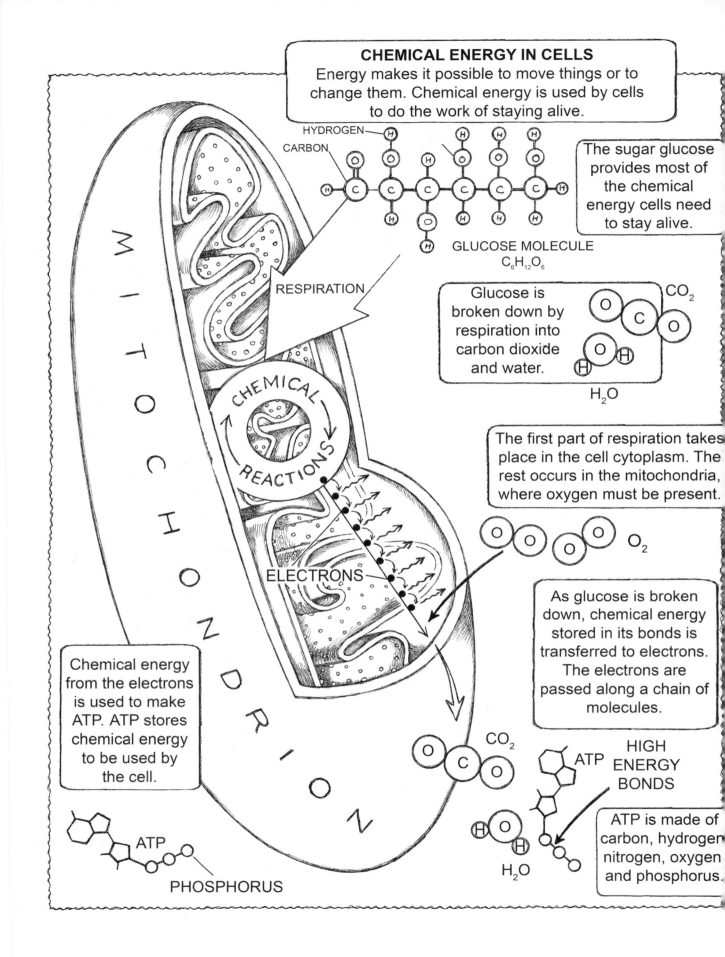

CHEMICAL ENERGY IN CELLS
Energy makes it possible to move things or to change them. Chemical energy is used by cells to do the work of staying alive.

HYDROGEN

CARBON

GLUCOSE MOLECULE
$C_6H_{12}O_6$

The sugar glucose provides most of the chemical energy cells need to stay alive.

Glucose is broken down by respiration into carbon dioxide and water.

CO_2

H_2O

RESPIRATION

CHEMICAL REACTIONS

The first part of respiration takes place in the cell cytoplasm. The rest occurs in the mitochondria, where oxygen must be present.

O_2

ELECTRONS

As glucose is broken down, chemical energy stored in its bonds is transferred to electrons. The electrons are passed along a chain of molecules.

Chemical energy from the electrons is used to make ATP. ATP stores chemical energy to be used by the cell.

MITOCHONDRION

CO_2

ATP

HIGH ENERGY BONDS

H_2O

ATP

PHOSPHORUS

ATP is made of carbon, hydrogen, nitrogen, oxygen and phosphorus.

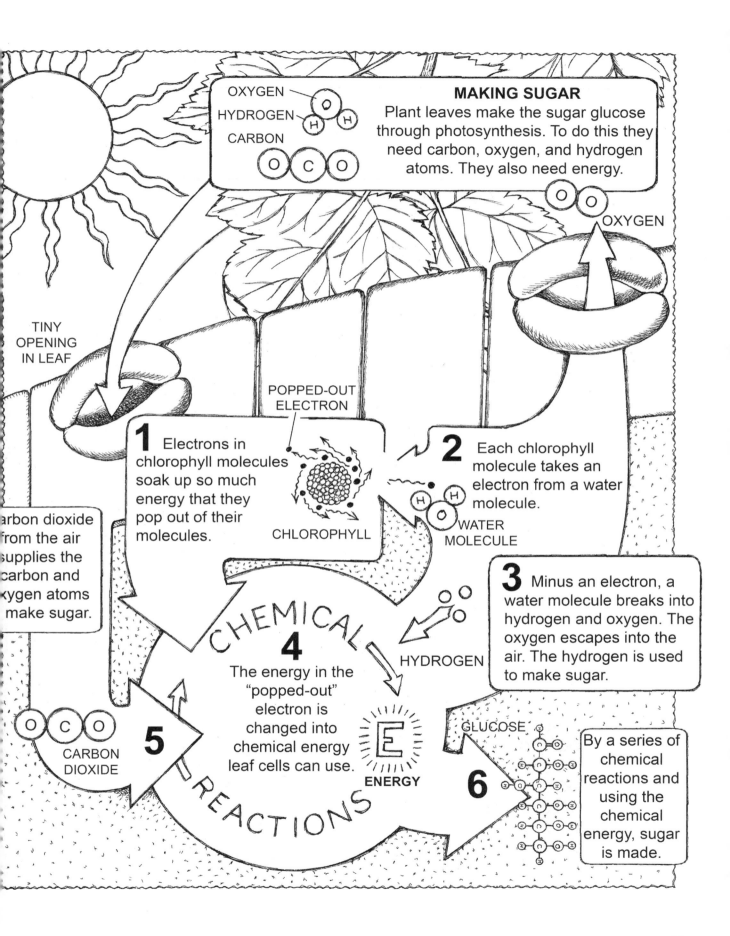

OXYGEN

HYDROGEN

CARBON

MAKING SUGAR
Plant leaves make the sugar glucose through photosynthesis. To do this they need carbon, oxygen, and hydrogen atoms. They also need energy.

OXYGEN

TINY
OPENING
IN LEAF

POPPED-OUT
ELECTRON

1 Electrons in chlorophyll molecules soak up so much energy that they pop out of their molecules.

CHLOROPHYLL

2 Each chlorophyll molecule takes an electron from a water molecule.

WATER
MOLECULE

arbon dioxide from the air supplies the carbon and xygen atoms make sugar.

3 Minus an electron, a water molecule breaks into hydrogen and oxygen. The oxygen escapes into the air. The hydrogen is used to make sugar.

CHEMICAL

4 The energy in the "popped-out" electron is changed into chemical energy leaf cells can use.

HYDROGEN

ENERGY

CARBON
DIOXIDE

5

REACTIONS

GLUCOSE

6 By a series of chemical reactions and using the chemical energy, sugar is made.

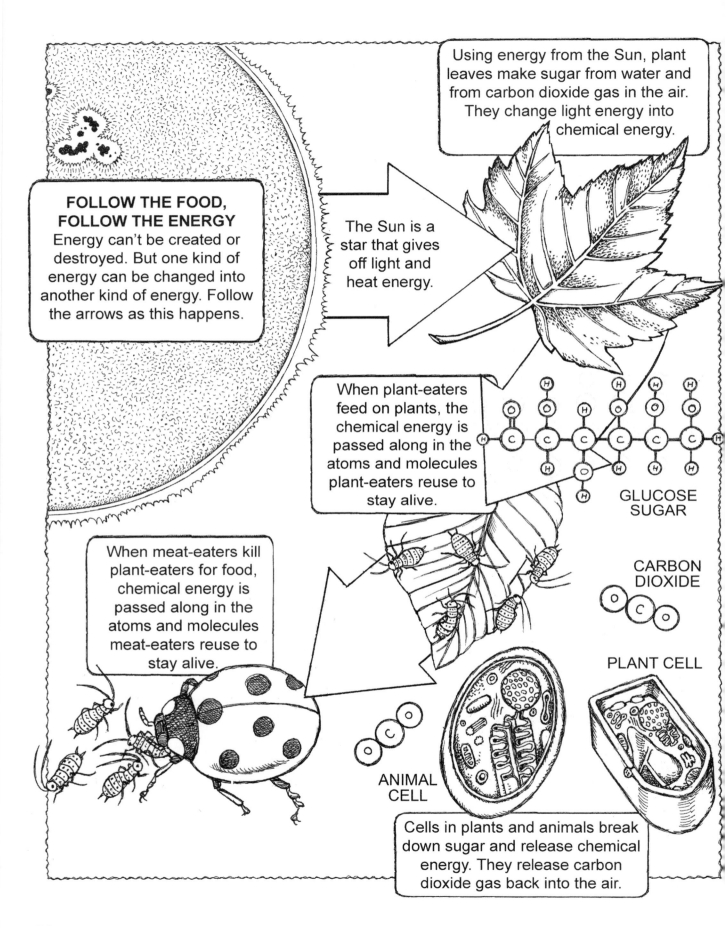

Using energy from the Sun, plant leaves make sugar from water and from carbon dioxide gas in the air. They change light energy into chemical energy.

FOLLOW THE FOOD, FOLLOW THE ENERGY
Energy can't be created or destroyed. But one kind of energy can be changed into another kind of energy. Follow the arrows as this happens.

The Sun is a star that gives off light and heat energy.

When plant-eaters feed on plants, the chemical energy is passed along in the atoms and molecules plant-eaters reuse to stay alive.

GLUCOSE SUGAR

CARBON DIOXIDE

When meat-eaters kill plant-eaters for food, chemical energy is passed along in the atoms and molecules meat-eaters reuse to stay alive.

PLANT CELL

ANIMAL CELL

Cells in plants and animals break down sugar and release chemical energy. They release carbon dioxide gas back into the air.

24

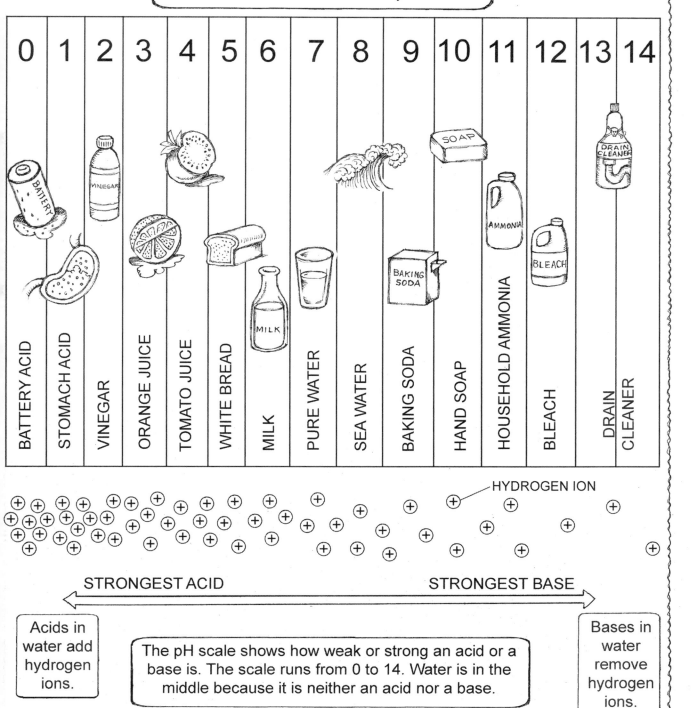

ACIDS AND BASES
Weak acids in orange juice won't hurt you. Nor will weak bases in hand soap. But stay away from strong acids and bases. They can make holes in metal and burn your skin.

0	1	2	3	4	5	6	7	8	9	10	11	12	13	14

BATTERY ACID · STOMACH ACID · VINEGAR · ORANGE JUICE · TOMATO JUICE · WHITE BREAD · MILK · PURE WATER · SEA WATER · BAKING SODA · HAND SOAP · HOUSEHOLD AMMONIA · BLEACH · DRAIN CLEANER

HYDROGEN ION

STRONGEST ACID   STRONGEST BASE

Acids in water add hydrogen ions.

The pH scale shows how weak or strong an acid or a base is. The scale runs from 0 to 14. Water is in the middle because it is neither an acid nor a base.

Bases in water remove hydrogen ions.

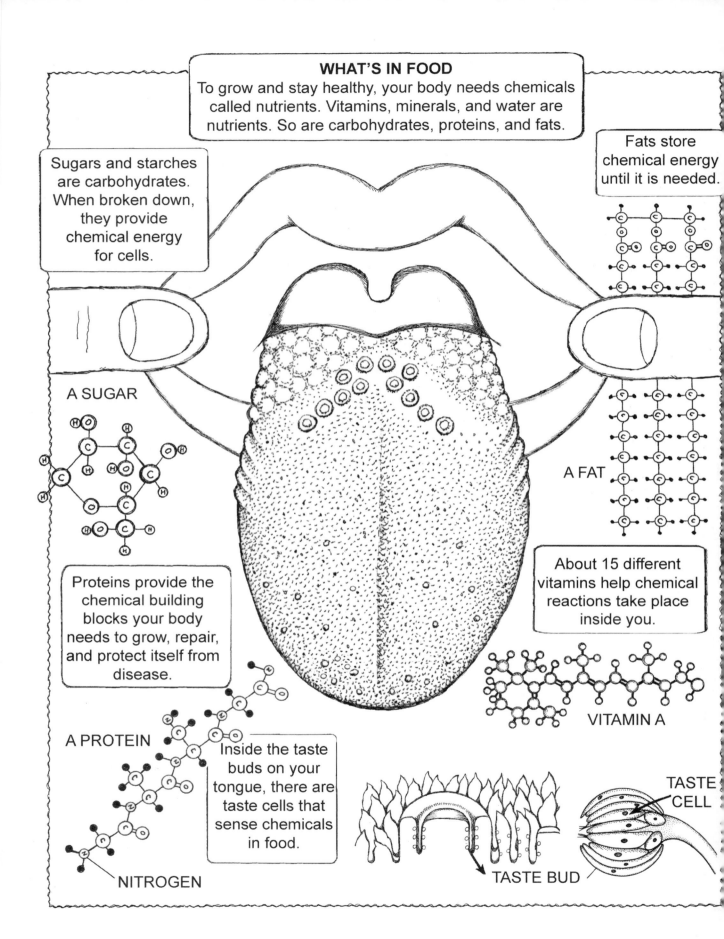

WHAT'S IN FOOD
To grow and stay healthy, your body needs chemicals called nutrients. Vitamins, minerals, and water are nutrients. So are carbohydrates, proteins, and fats.

Sugars and starches are carbohydrates. When broken down, they provide chemical energy for cells.

Fats store chemical energy until it is needed.

A SUGAR

A FAT

Proteins provide the chemical building blocks your body needs to grow, repair, and protect itself from disease.

About 15 different vitamins help chemical reactions take place inside you.

VITAMIN A

A PROTEIN

Inside the taste buds on your tongue, there are taste cells that sense chemicals in food.

NITROGEN

TASTE BUD

TASTE CELL

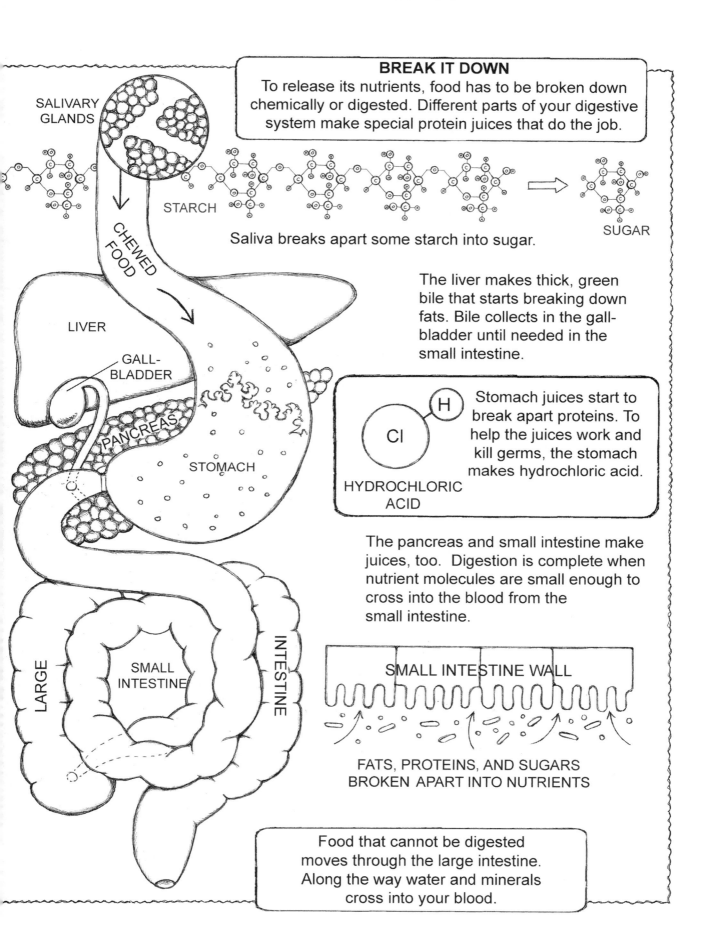

SALIVARY
GLANDS

BREAK IT DOWN
To release its nutrients, food has to be broken down
chemically or digested. Different parts of your digestive
system make special protein juices that do the job.

STARCH

SUGAR

Saliva breaks apart some starch into sugar.

CHEWED FOOD

The liver makes thick, green
bile that starts breaking down
fats. Bile collects in the gall-
bladder until needed in the
small intestine.

LIVER

GALL-
BLADDER

PANCREAS

STOMACH

Stomach juices start to
break apart proteins. To
help the juices work and
kill germs, the stomach
makes hydrochloric acid.

H

Cl

HYDROCHLORIC
ACID

The pancreas and small intestine make
juices, too. Digestion is complete when
nutrient molecules are small enough to
cross into the blood from the
small intestine.

LARGE

SMALL
INTESTINE

INTESTINE

SMALL INTESTINE WALL

FATS, PROTEINS, AND SUGARS
BROKEN APART INTO NUTRIENTS

Food that cannot be digested
moves through the large intestine.
Along the way water and minerals
cross into your blood.

BREATHING GASES IN, BREATHING GASES OUT

Breathe in: your body just took in the gases in the air around you. Breathe out: something has changed. There is less oxygen and more carbon dioxide.

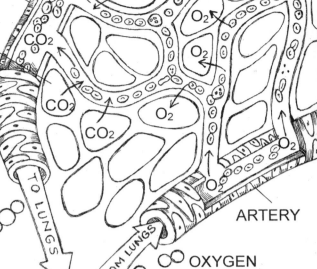

VEIN

BODY CELL

CO_2

CO_2

CO_2

CO_2

O_2

O_2

O_2

O_2

O_2

TO LUNGS

FROM LUNGS

ARTERY

ALVEOLI

Your blood picks up waste carbon dioxide from cells and carries it back to your lungs.

CARBON DIOXIDE MOLECULES

OXYGEN MOLECULES

In your lungs are tiny air sacs called alveoli. Oxygen from the air passes out of the sacs and into your blood. Waste carbon dioxide goes the other way.

Cells need oxygen to use the chemica[l] energy from broken-down sugar. When [c] work they produce carbon dioxide. To[o] much carbon dioxide is harmful to cell[s]

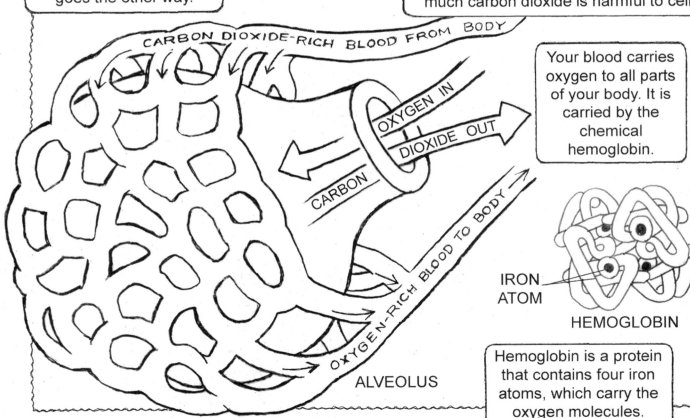

CARBON DIOXIDE-RICH BLOOD FROM BODY

OXYGEN IN

CARBON DIOXIDE OUT

OXYGEN-RICH BLOOD TO BODY

ALVEOLUS

Your blood carries oxygen to all parts of your body. It is carried by the chemical hemoglobin.

IRON ATOM

HEMOGLOBIN

Hemoglobin is a protein that contains four iron atoms, which carry the oxygen molecules.

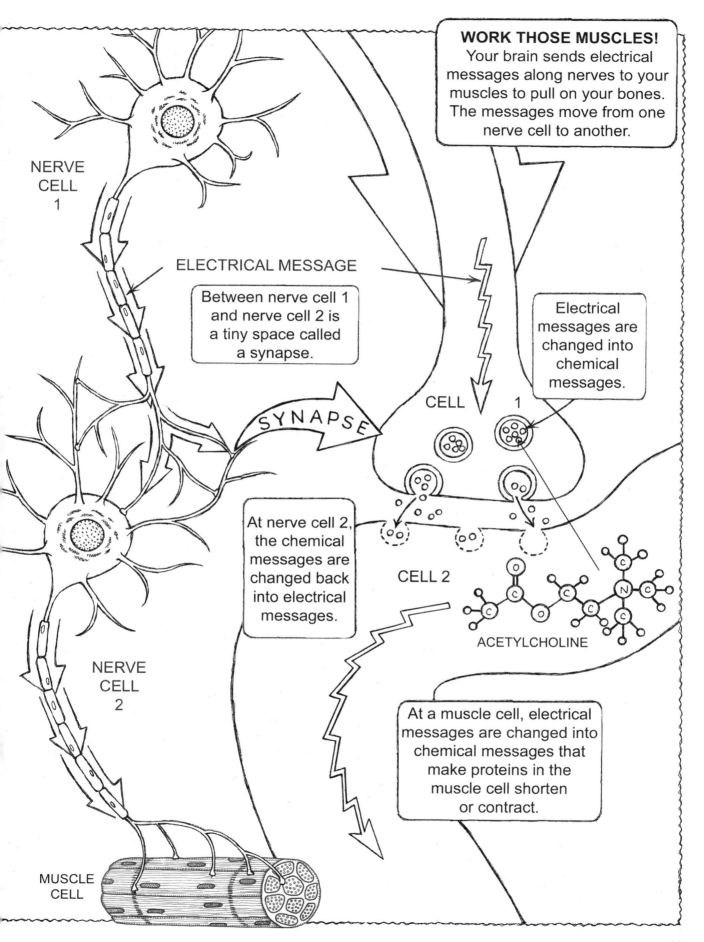

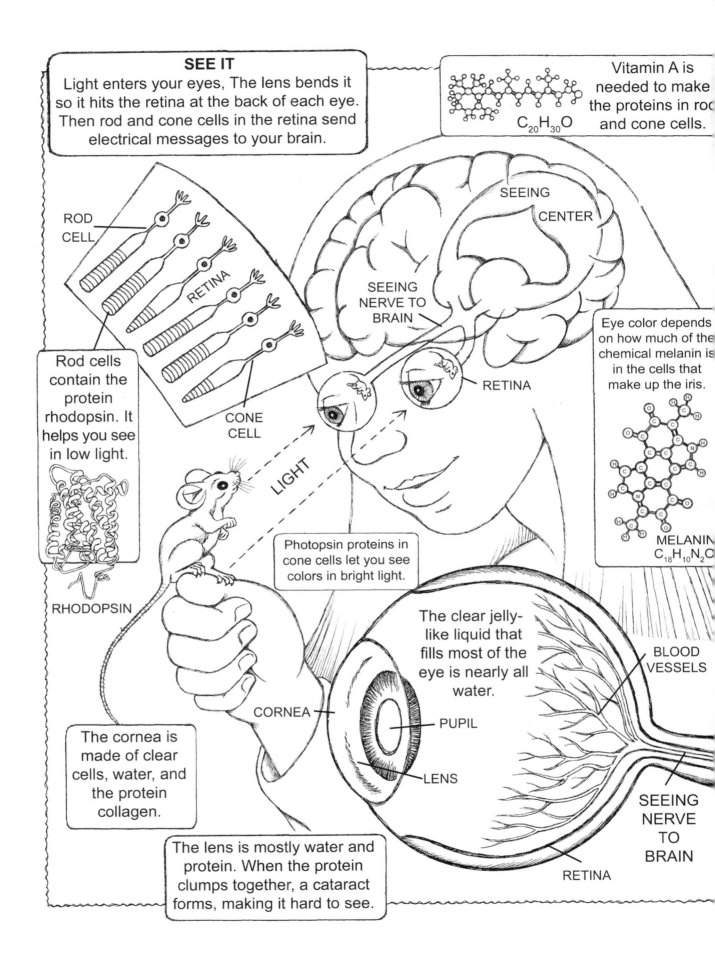

SEE IT
Light enters your eyes, The lens bends it so it hits the retina at the back of each eye. Then rod and cone cells in the retina send electrical messages to your brain.

Vitamin A is needed to make the proteins in rod and cone cells.

$C_{20}H_{30}O$

ROD CELL

RETINA

CONE CELL

Rod cells contain the protein rhodopsin. It helps you see in low light.

RHODOPSIN

SEEING CENTER

SEEING NERVE TO BRAIN

RETINA

Eye color depends on how much of the chemical melanin is in the cells that make up the iris.

MELANIN
$C_{18}H_{10}N_2O$

Photopsin proteins in cone cells let you see colors in bright light.

LIGHT

The clear jelly-like liquid that fills most of the eye is nearly all water.

BLOOD VESSELS

CORNEA

PUPIL

LENS

The cornea is made of clear cells, water, and the protein collagen.

The lens is mostly water and protein. When the protein clumps together, a cataract forms, making it hard to see.

SEEING NERVE TO BRAIN

RETINA

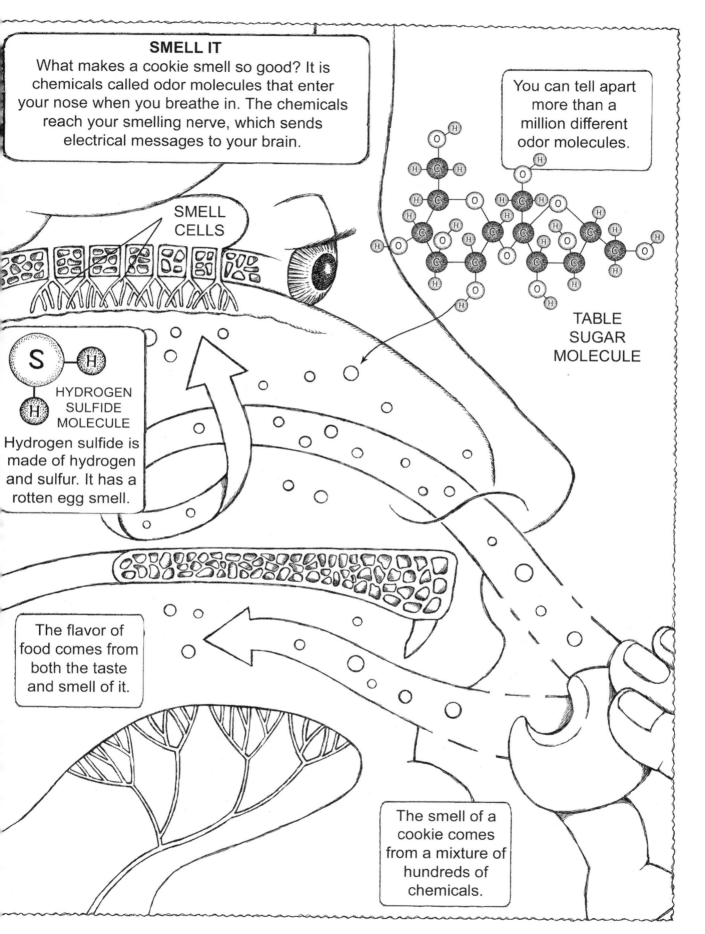

SMELL IT
What makes a cookie smell so good? It is chemicals called odor molecules that enter your nose when you breathe in. The chemicals reach your smelling nerve, which sends electrical messages to your brain.

You can tell apart more than a million different odor molecules.

SMELL CELLS

TABLE SUGAR MOLECULE

S — H

H

HYDROGEN SULFIDE MOLECULE

Hydrogen sulfide is made of hydrogen and sulfur. It has a rotten egg smell.

The flavor of food comes from both the taste and smell of it.

The smell of a cookie comes from a mixture of hundreds of chemicals.

31

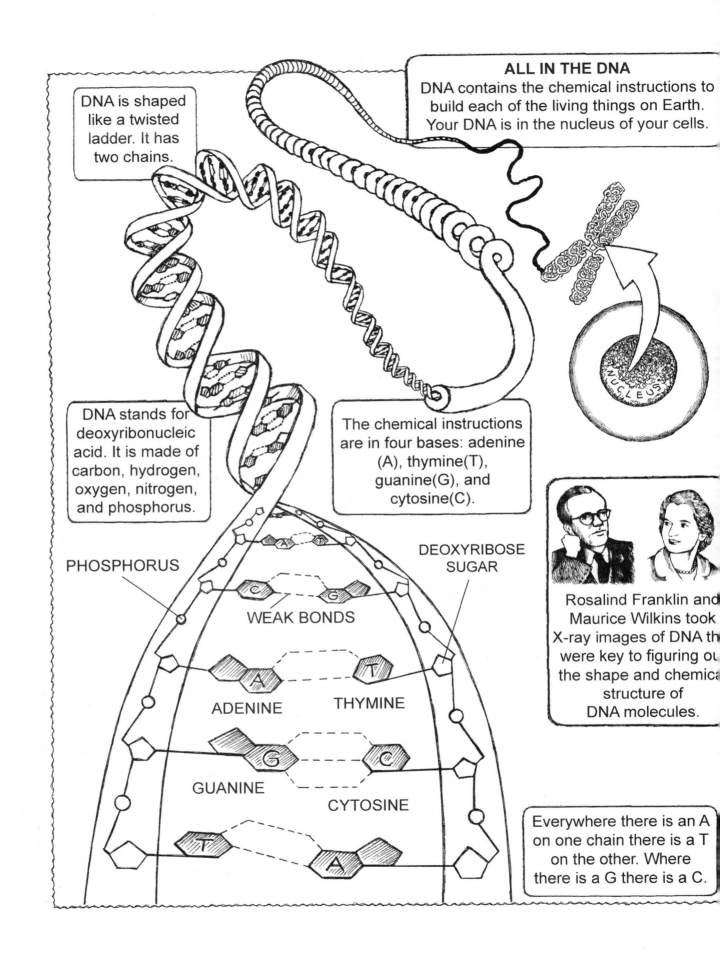

ALL IN THE DNA
DNA contains the chemical instructions to build each of the living things on Earth. Your DNA is in the nucleus of your cells.

DNA is shaped like a twisted ladder. It has two chains.

DNA stands for deoxyribonucleic acid. It is made of carbon, hydrogen, oxygen, nitrogen, and phosphorus.

The chemical instructions are in four bases: adenine (A), thymine(T), guanine(G), and cytosine(C).

Rosalind Franklin and Maurice Wilkins took X-ray images of DNA th were key to figuring ou the shape and chemica structure of DNA molecules.

PHOSPHORUS

DEOXYRIBOSE SUGAR

WEAK BONDS

ADENINE

THYMINE

GUANINE

CYTOSINE

Everywhere there is an A on one chain there is a T on the other. Where there is a G there is a C.

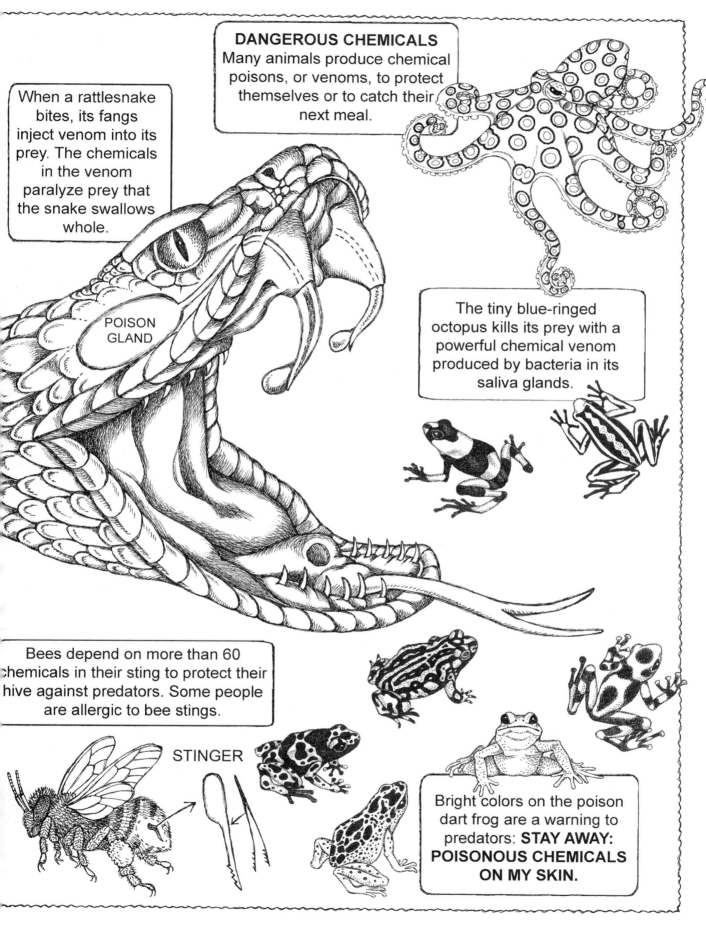

DANGEROUS CHEMICALS
Many animals produce chemical poisons, or venoms, to protect themselves or to catch their next meal.

When a rattlesnake bites, its fangs inject venom into its prey. The chemicals in the venom paralyze prey that the snake swallows whole.

POISON GLAND

The tiny blue-ringed octopus kills its prey with a powerful chemical venom produced by bacteria in its saliva glands.

Bees depend on more than 60 chemicals in their sting to protect their hive against predators. Some people are allergic to bee stings.

STINGER

Bright colors on the poison dart frog are a warning to predators: **STAY AWAY: POISONOUS CHEMICALS ON MY SKIN.**

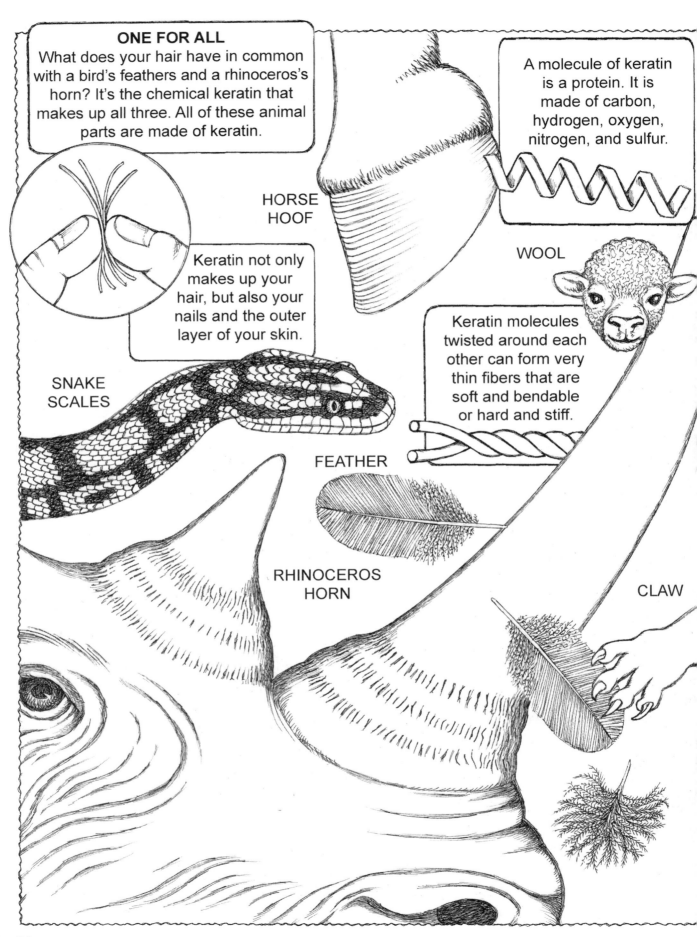

ONE FOR ALL
What does your hair have in common with a bird's feathers and a rhinoceros's horn? It's the chemical keratin that makes up all three. All of these animal parts are made of keratin.

A molecule of keratin is a protein. It is made of carbon, hydrogen, oxygen, nitrogen, and sulfur.

HORSE HOOF

WOOL

Keratin not only makes up your hair, but also your nails and the outer layer of your skin.

Keratin molecules twisted around each other can form very thin fibers that are soft and bendable or hard and stiff.

SNAKE SCALES

FEATHER

RHINOCEROS HORN

CLAW

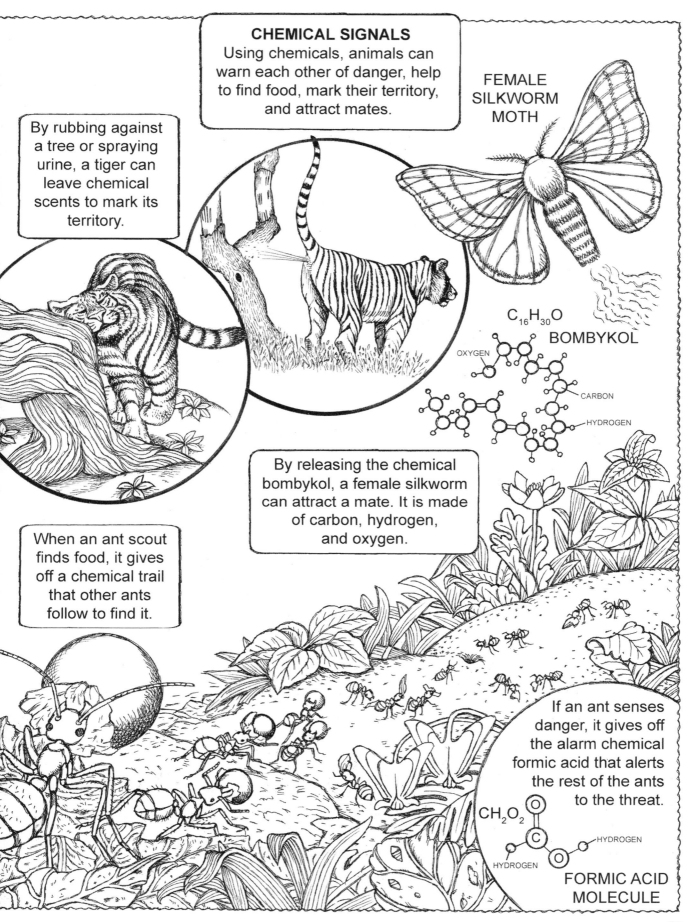

CHEMICAL SIGNALS
Using chemicals, animals can warn each other of danger, help to find food, mark their territory, and attract mates.

By rubbing against a tree or spraying urine, a tiger can leave chemical scents to mark its territory.

FEMALE SILKWORM MOTH

$C_{16}H_{30}O$
BOMBYKOL

OXYGEN

CARBON

HYDROGEN

By releasing the chemical bombykol, a female silkworm can attract a mate. It is made of carbon, hydrogen, and oxygen.

When an ant scout finds food, it gives off a chemical trail that other ants follow to find it.

If an ant senses danger, it gives off the alarm chemical formic acid that alerts the rest of the ants to the threat.

CH_2O_2

HYDROGEN

HYDROGEN

FORMIC ACID MOLECULE

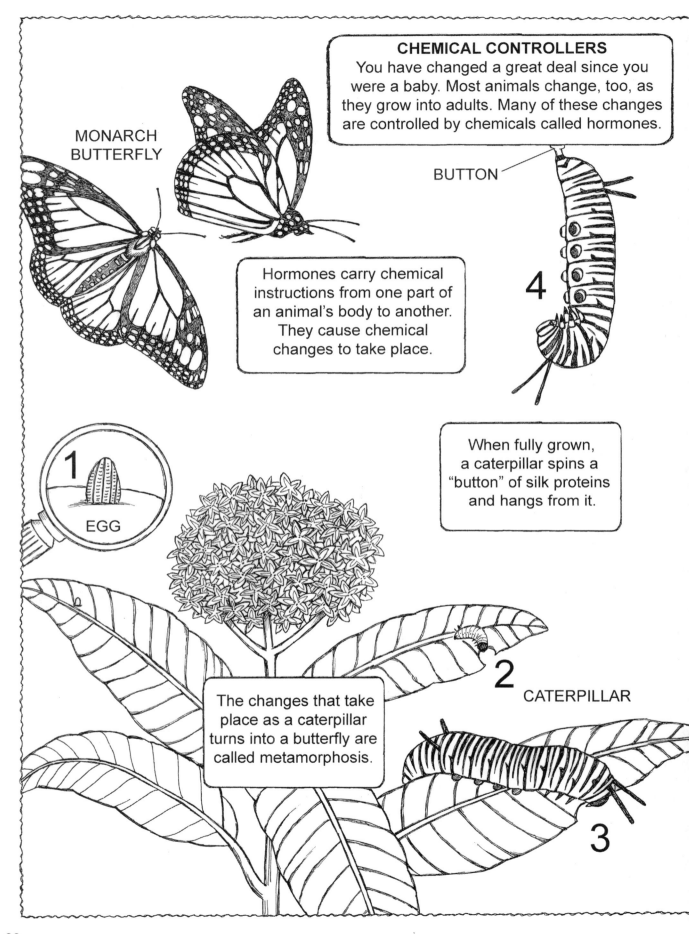

CHEMICAL CONTROLLERS
You have changed a great deal since you were a baby. Most animals change, too, as they grow into adults. Many of these changes are controlled by chemicals called hormones.

MONARCH BUTTERFLY

BUTTON

Hormones carry chemical instructions from one part of an animal's body to another. They cause chemical changes to take place.

4

When fully grown, a caterpillar spins a "button" of silk proteins and hangs from it.

1
EGG

The changes that take place as a caterpillar turns into a butterfly are called metamorphosis.

2
CATERPILLAR

3

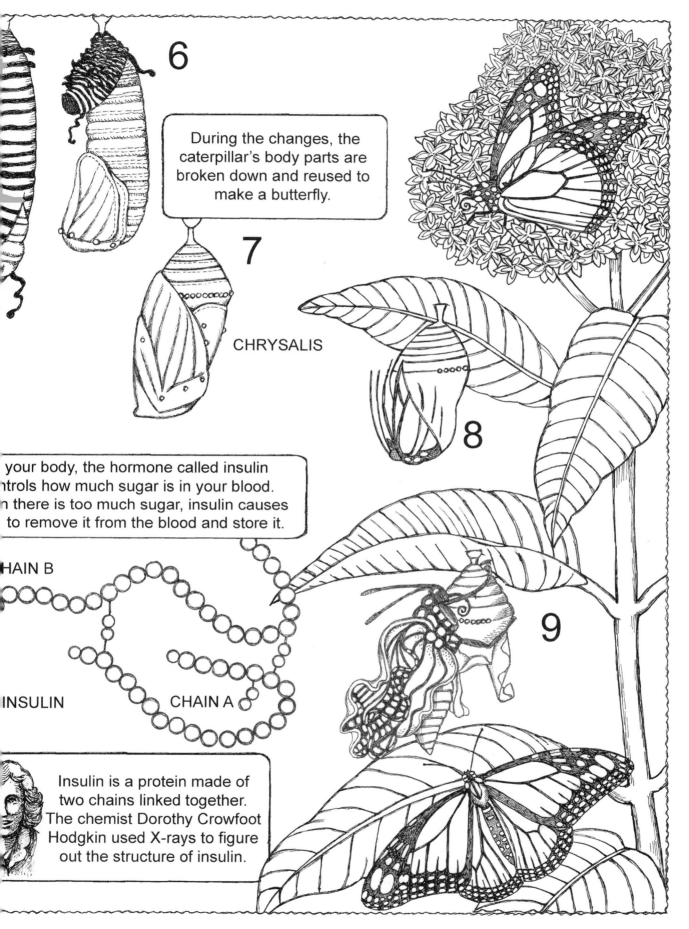

6

During the changes, the caterpillar's body parts are broken down and reused to make a butterfly.

7

CHRYSALIS

8

your body, the hormone called insulin
ntrols how much sugar is in your blood.
n there is too much sugar, insulin causes
to remove it from the blood and store it.

HAIN B

INSULIN   CHAIN A

9

Insulin is a protein made of
two chains linked together.
The chemist Dorothy Crowfoot
Hodgkin used X-rays to figure
out the structure of insulin.

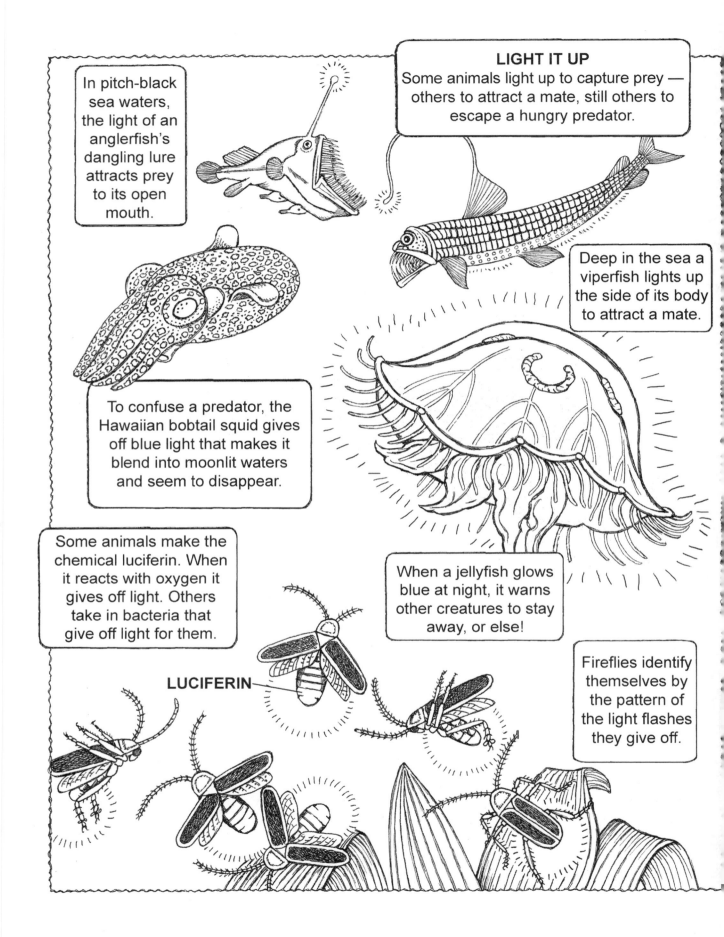

In pitch-black sea waters, the light of an anglerfish's dangling lure attracts prey to its open mouth.

LIGHT IT UP
Some animals light up to capture prey — others to attract a mate, still others to escape a hungry predator.

Deep in the sea a viperfish lights up the side of its body to attract a mate.

To confuse a predator, the Hawaiian bobtail squid gives off blue light that makes it blend into moonlit waters and seem to disappear.

Some animals make the chemical luciferin. When it reacts with oxygen it gives off light. Others take in bacteria that give off light for them.

LUCIFERIN

When a jellyfish glows blue at night, it warns other creatures to stay away, or else!

Fireflies identify themselves by the pattern of the light flashes they give off.

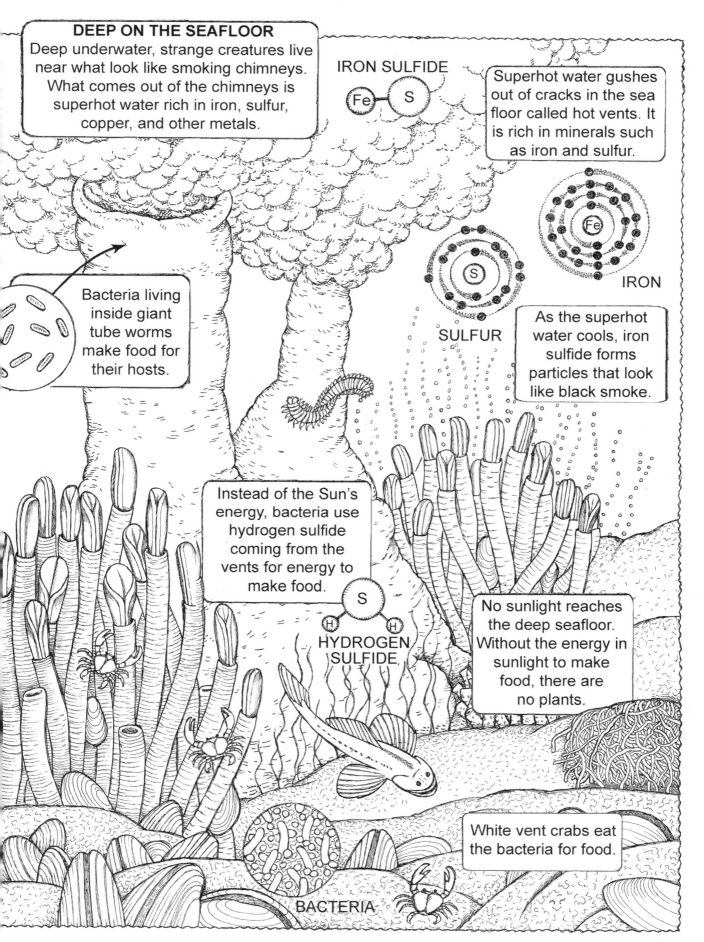

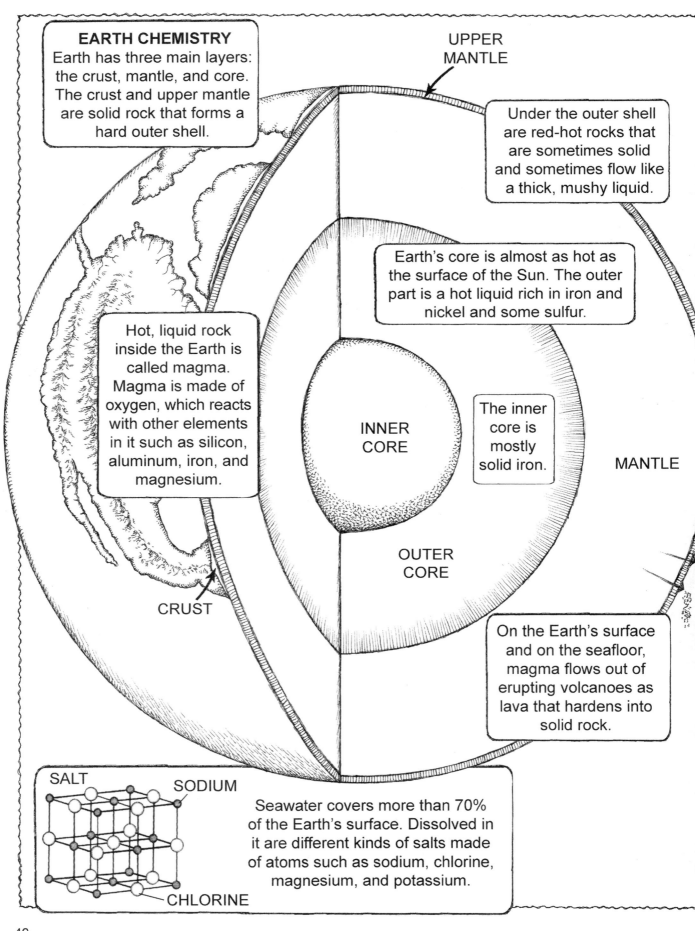

EARTH CHEMISTRY
Earth has three main layers: the crust, mantle, and core. The crust and upper mantle are solid rock that forms a hard outer shell.

UPPER MANTLE

Under the outer shell are red-hot rocks that are sometimes solid and sometimes flow like a thick, mushy liquid.

Earth's core is almost as hot as the surface of the Sun. The outer part is a hot liquid rich in iron and nickel and some sulfur.

Hot, liquid rock inside the Earth is called magma. Magma is made of oxygen, which reacts with other elements in it such as silicon, aluminum, iron, and magnesium.

INNER CORE

The inner core is mostly solid iron.

MANTLE

CRUST

OUTER CORE

On the Earth's surface and on the seafloor, magma flows out of erupting volcanoes as lava that hardens into solid rock.

SALT

SODIUM

Seawater covers more than 70% of the Earth's surface. Dissolved in it are different kinds of salts made of atoms such as sodium, chlorine, magnesium, and potassium.

CHLORINE

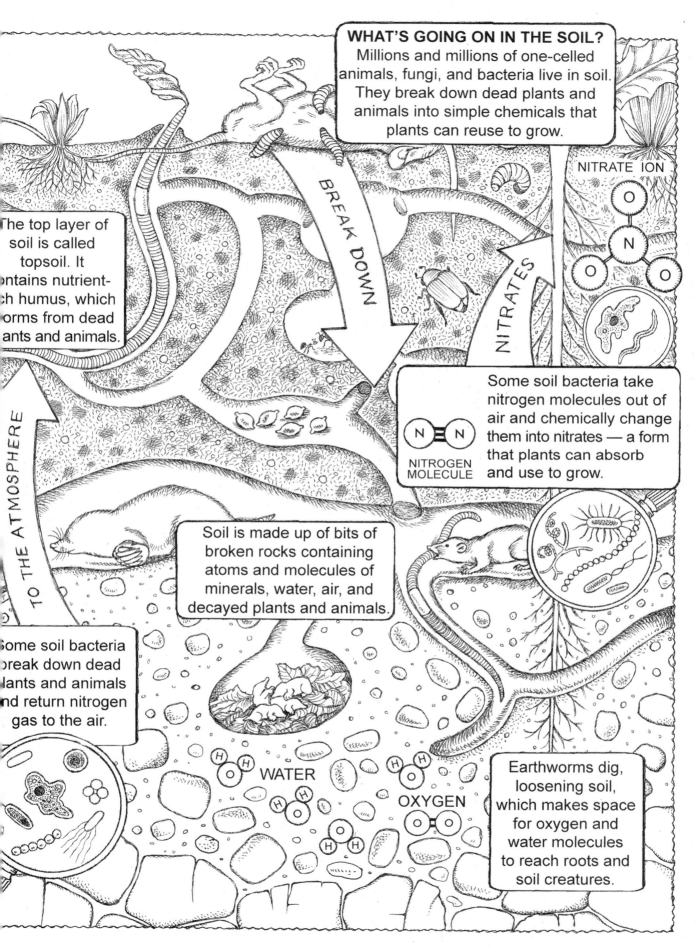

WHAT'S GOING ON IN THE SOIL?
Millions and millions of one-celled animals, fungi, and bacteria live in soil. They break down dead plants and animals into simple chemicals that plants can reuse to grow.

NITRATE ION

BREAK DOWN

NITRATES

The top layer of soil is called topsoil. It contains nutrient-rich humus, which forms from dead plants and animals.

Some soil bacteria take nitrogen molecules out of air and chemically change them into nitrates — a form that plants can absorb and use to grow.

NITROGEN MOLECULE

TO THE ATMOSPHERE

Soil is made up of bits of broken rocks containing atoms and molecules of minerals, water, air, and decayed plants and animals.

Some soil bacteria break down dead plants and animals and return nitrogen gas to the air.

WATER

OXYGEN

Earthworms dig, loosening soil, which makes space for oxygen and water molecules to reach roots and soil creatures.

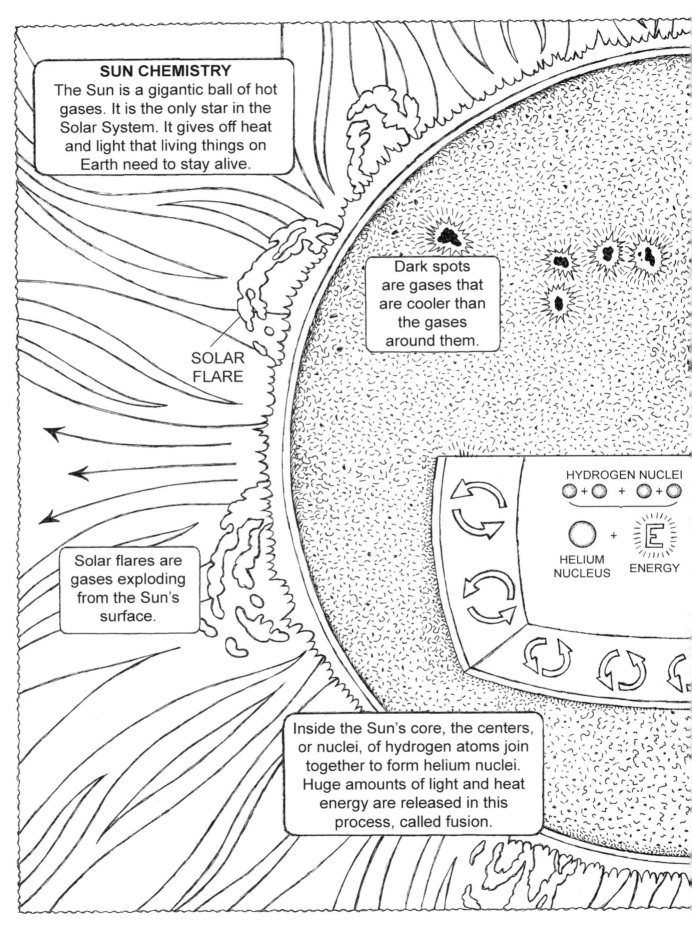

SUN CHEMISTRY
The Sun is a gigantic ball of hot gases. It is the only star in the Solar System. It gives off heat and light that living things on Earth need to stay alive.

Dark spots are gases that are cooler than the gases around them.

SOLAR FLARE

Solar flares are gases exploding from the Sun's surface.

HYDROGEN NUCLEI

HELIUM NUCLEUS

ENERGY

Inside the Sun's core, the centers, or nuclei, of hydrogen atoms join together to form helium nuclei. Huge amounts of light and heat energy are released in this process, called fusion.

1

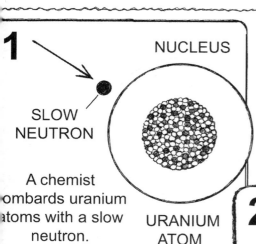

NUCLEUS

SLOW NEUTRON

A chemist bombards uranium atoms with a slow neutron.

URANIUM ATOM

SPLITTING APART A NUCLEUS
The nuclei of most atoms are firmly packed together. But the nuclei of large atoms such as uranium are not. They give off particles and harmful rays. These atoms are radioactive.
Follow the numbers to find out how the nucleus of a uranium atom is split apart by the process of fission.

2

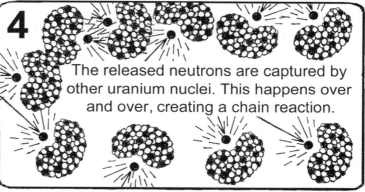

The nucleus of a uranium atom captures a neutron and splits apart.

3

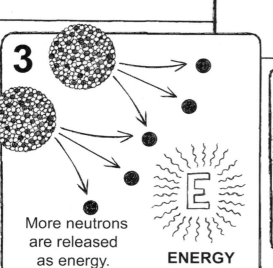

More neutrons are released as energy.

E

ENERGY

4

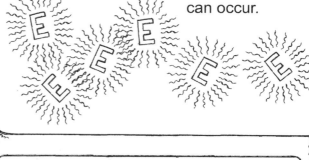

The released neutrons are captured by other uranium nuclei. This happens over and over, creating a chain reaction.

5 A tremendous amount of energy is released. If the chain reaction isn't stopped, a massive explosion can occur.

In a nuclear power plant, uranium atoms are split into smaller atoms so that heat energy is slowly released. The heat energy is used to produce electricity for cities and towns.

Marie Curie and her husband discovered the radioactive elements polonium and radium.

43

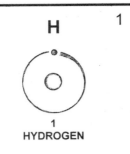

H 1

1
HYDROGEN

ALL TOGETHER

Elements can be grouped together based on their properties to form a periodic table. In this table, elements under each other have similar, but not identical, properties. Except for hydrogen, the properties of elements from left to right in each row change from metals, to metalloids, to nonmetals.

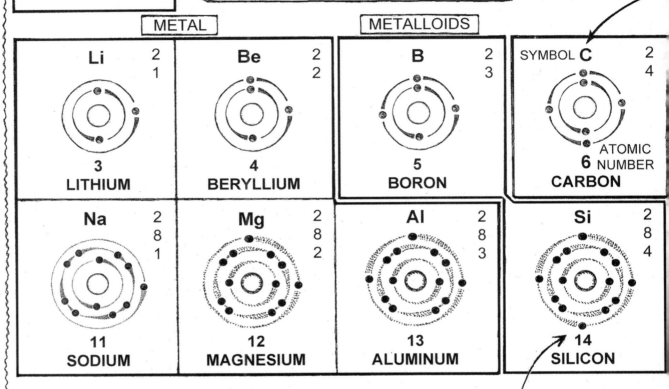

METAL

METALLOIDS

Li 2 1

3
LITHIUM

Be 2 2

4
BERYLLIUM

B 2 3

5
BORON

SYMBOL **C** 2 4

ATOMIC
6 NUMBER
CARBON

Na 2 8 1

11
SODIUM

Mg 2 8 2

12
MAGNESIUM

Al 2 8 3

13
ALUMINUM

Si 2 8 4

14
SILICON

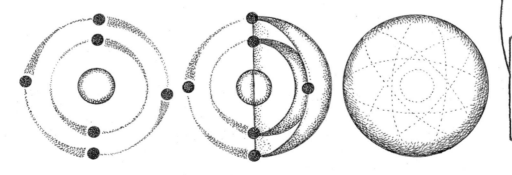

The number of electrons in each element is the same as the number of protons.

There are three ways to show a carbon atom. On the left there are 6 electrons whizzing around the nucleus of the atom. In the middle, a section of the carbon atom has been removed. Most of the atom is empty space. On the right the whizzing electrons create an energy cloud around the nucleus.

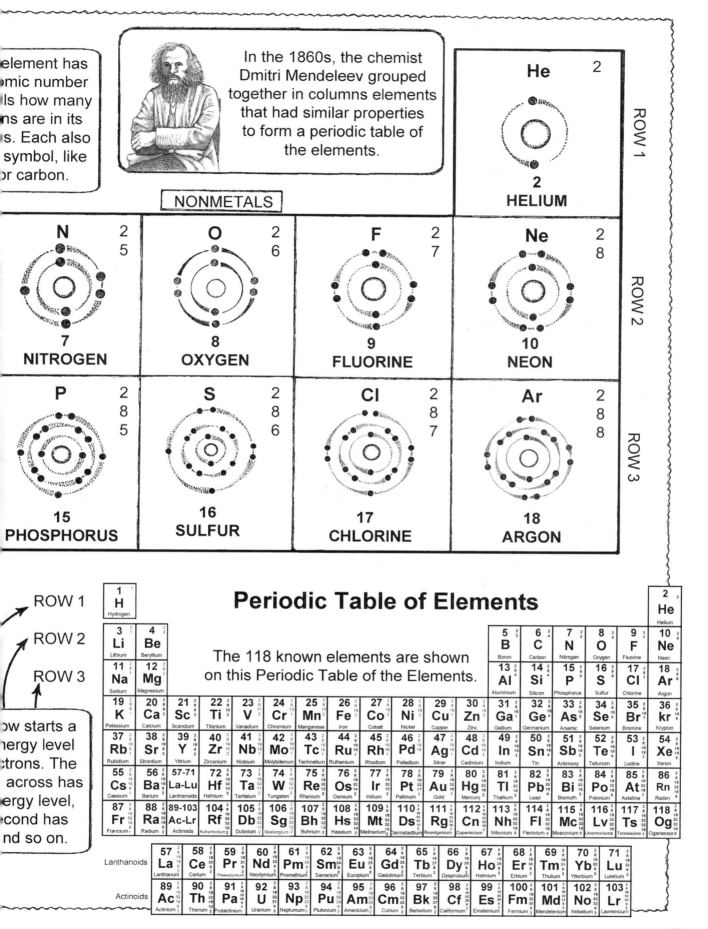

element has
omic number
lls how many
ns are in its
s. Each also
symbol, like
r carbon.

In the 1860s, the chemist Dmitri Mendeleev grouped together in columns elements that had similar properties to form a periodic table of the elements.

He 2

2
HELIUM

ROW 1

NONMETALS

N 2 5	O 2 6	F 2 7	Ne 2 8
7 NITROGEN	8 OXYGEN	9 FLUORINE	10 NEON

ROW 2

P 2 8 5	S 2 8 6	Cl 2 8 7	Ar 2 8 8
15 PHOSPHORUS	16 SULFUR	17 CHLORINE	18 ARGON

ROW 3

ROW 1
ROW 2
ROW 3

ow starts a
ergy level
ctrons. The
across has
ergy level,
cond has
nd so on.

Periodic Table of Elements

The 118 known elements are shown on this Periodic Table of the Elements.

1 H Hydrogen																	2 He Helium
3 Li Lithium	4 Be Beryllium											5 B Boron	6 C Carbon	7 N Nitrogen	8 O Oxygen	9 F Fluorine	10 Ne Neon
11 Na Sodium	12 Mg Magnesium											13 Al Aluminium	14 Si Silicon	15 P Phosphorus	16 S Sulfur	17 Cl Chlorine	18 Ar Argon
19 K Potassium	20 Ca Calcium	21 Sc Scandium	22 Ti Titanium	23 V Vanadium	24 Cr Chromium	25 Mn Manganese	26 Fe Iron	27 Co Cobalt	28 Ni Nickel	29 Cu Copper	30 Zn Zinc	31 Ga Gallium	32 Ge Germanium	33 As Arsenic	34 Se Selenium	35 Br Bromine	36 kr Krypton
37 Rb Rubidium	38 Sr Strontium	39 Y Yttrium	40 Zr Zirconium	41 Nb Niobium	42 Mo Molybdenum	43 Tc Technetium	44 Ru Ruthenium	45 Rh Rhodium	46 Pd Palladium	47 Ag Silver	48 Cd Cadmium	49 In Indium	50 Sn Tin	51 Sb Antimony	52 Te Tellurium	53 I Iodine	54 Xe Xenon
55 Cs Caesium	56 Ba Barium	57-71 La-Lu Lanthanoids	72 Hf Hafnium	73 Ta Tantalum	74 W Tungsten	75 Re Rhenium	76 Os Osmium	77 Ir Iridium	78 Pt Paltinum	79 Au Gold	80 Hg Mercury	81 Tl Thallium	82 Pb Lead	83 Bi Bismuth	84 Po Polonium	85 At Astatine	86 Rn Radon
87 Fr Francium	88 Ra Radium	89-103 Ac-Lr Actinoids	104 Rf Rutherfordium	105 Db Dubnium	106 Sg Seaborgium	107 Bh Bohrium	108 Hs Hassium	109 Mt Meitnerium	110 Ds Darmstadtium	111 Rg Roentgenium	112 Cn Copernicium	113 Nh Nihonium	114 Fl Flerovium	115 Mc Moscovium	116 Lv Livermorium	117 Ts Tennessine	118 Og Oganesson

Lanthanoids	57 La Lanthanum	58 Ce Cerium	59 Pr Praseodymium	60 Nd Neodymium	61 Pm Promethium	62 Sm Samarium	63 Eu Europium	64 Gd Gadolinium	65 Tb Terbium	66 Dy Dysprosium	67 Ho Holmium	68 Er Erbium	69 Tm Thulium	70 Yb Ytterbium	71 Lu Lutetium
Actinoids	89 Ac Actinium	90 Th Thorium	91 Pa Protactinium	92 U Uranium	93 Np Neptunium	94 Pu Plutonium	95 Am Americium	96 Cm Curium	97 Bk Berkelium	98 Cf Californium	99 Es Einsteinium	100 Fm Fermium	101 Md Mendelevium	102 No Nobelium	103 Lr Lawrencium

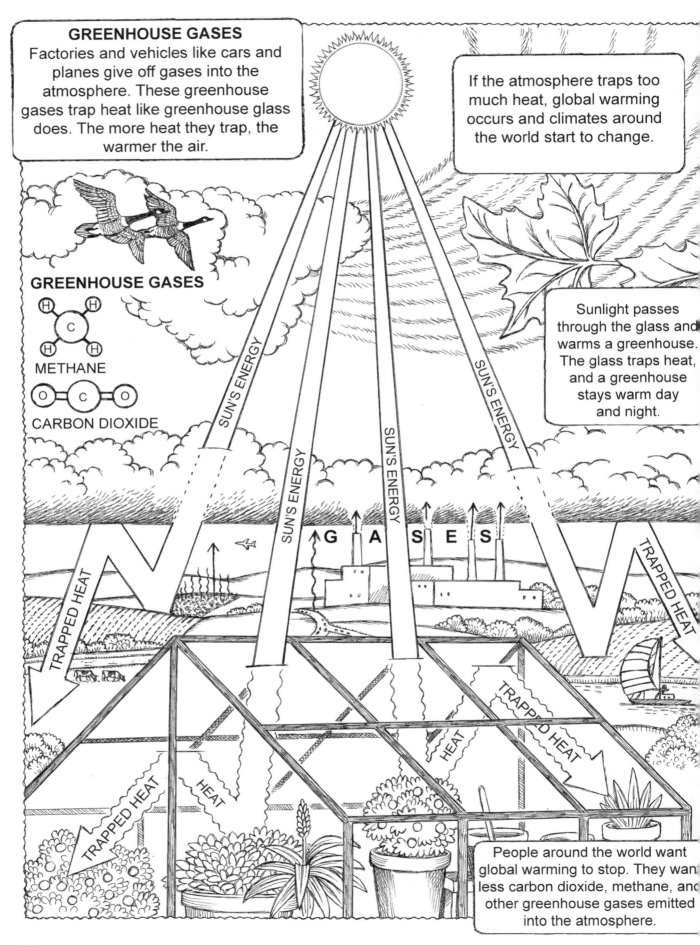

GREENHOUSE GASES
Factories and vehicles like cars and planes give off gases into the atmosphere. These greenhouse gases trap heat like greenhouse glass does. The more heat they trap, the warmer the air.

If the atmosphere traps too much heat, global warming occurs and climates around the world start to change.

GREENHOUSE GASES

METHANE

CARBON DIOXIDE

Sunlight passes through the glass and warms a greenhouse. The glass traps heat, and a greenhouse stays warm day and night.

SUN'S ENERGY

GASES

TRAPPED HEAT

HEAT

People around the world want global warming to stop. They want less carbon dioxide, methane, and other greenhouse gases emitted into the atmosphere.